SUDDENLY SINGLE

Money Skills for Divorcées and Widows

KERRY HANNON

JOHN WILEY & SONS, INC.

New York • Chichester • Weinheim • Brisbane • Singapore • Toronto

This book is printed on acid-free paper. ∞

Copyright © 1998 by Kerry Hannon. All rights reserved.
Published by John Wiley & Sons, Inc.

Published simultaneously in Canada.

Library of Congress Cataloging-in-Publication Data:

Hannon, Kerry.
    Suddenly single : money skills for divorcées and widows / by Kerry
Hannon.
        p.   cm.—(Wiley personal finance solutions)
    Includes index.
    ISBN 0-471-24311-6 (paper : alk. paper)
    1. Women—Finance, Personal.   2. Divorced women—Finance,
Personal.   3. Widows—Finance, Personal.   I. Title.   II. Series.
HG179.H256   1998
332.024′042—dc21   97-43071

Printed in the United States of America.

10 9 8 7 6 5 4 3 2 1

To my husband Cliff,
who taught me about managing money,
and to my parents,
who have always been an inspiration.

CONTENTS

$

INTRODUCTION

T he loss of a spouse is perhaps the most traumatic event imaginable. It's devastating in every sense of the word, regardless of whether you have been widowed or divorced. You say, "How can this be happening?" You're ripped apart inside. You're angry and lonely and scared. It's hard to think clearly, stop crying, and quit blaming yourself. Money is the last thing you want to think about.

Your world has suddenly changed forever, and having to deal with complicated money issues is benumbing. You just want to shut down, curl up in a ball, and pull the blanket over your head. You want someone else to handle things while you heal.

But you simply can't. For most women, that's a recipe for financial disaster. To rebuild your life, you need to get a grip on your finances as quickly as possible. That means figuring out your net worth and your sources of income, devising a budget you can live on comfortably, understanding your tax liabilities, pulling together a winning investing strategy, planning your retirement, and much more.

Many women never seriously think about their financial situation until they are left alone. And the consequences for such a do-nothing attitude can be dire. That's why you recognize the need to get information. And this book will help you take control of your finances.

Who will benefit from this book?

- Women who left money matters to their spouses or significant others and now find themselves on their own

- Women, now alone, who are unsure of their own decisions when it comes to money

- Women who confidently manage their own money, but are ignorant about how their departed husbands managed theirs

- Women who have never worked outside the home and are now on their own

- Single women who have been involved in a long-term, live-in relationship that has abruptly ended

- Women who are married, but suddenly can't rely financially on a spouse because he has lost his job or has become disabled

Finding yourself on your own after losing a man who helped support you, whether he was a husband, a father, or other loved one *is* scary, but you can get through it. The psychological and emotional issues are gut-wrenching. But becoming independent without a man as a financial partner in your life is almost as daunting. Both will take time. Making the effort to learn about money will give you the knowledge and confidence to handle your own finances. You will survive and flourish on your own. After all, financial security is personal freedom.

In the best of all worlds, you would be prepared before things collapse, but most of us aren't. However, with some planning, a slow, steady approach to investing, and careful budgeting, you'll be able to emerge from your loss with your financial world in order. This book is designed to help you get to that safe place.

You're not alone in having to cope with managing your money solo. Most women will be on their own one day. According to the National Center for Health Statistics, women live an average of seven years longer than men, and half of all women married in the past 20 years will eventually divorce. In fact, The National Center for Women and Retirement Research estimates that, all told, 80% to 90% of women will be solely responsible for their finances at some point in their lives.

Consider the following scenarios. If you're a typical woman, being on your own will result in a dramatic drop in your standard of living. Going from living comfortably on two incomes to trying to squeak by on one is tough, especially if you have children to support. Also, your salary is probably below your spouse's. Women between the ages of 35 and 44 still earn roughly 72 cents for every dollar a man makes. Women 45 to 55 make just 61 cents for every dollar earned by men. Furthermore,

- Only 15% of divorcing women are awarded any form of court-ordered spousal support these days. Of those women, 34% never receive a penny of what's due them.

- Fewer than half of all women awarded child support ever get the full amount to which they are entitled. The result: The typical woman's standard of living dives 45% in the first year of divorce while the average man's jumps 15%.

- Roughly 80% of widows now living in poverty were not poor before their husbands died, according to the General Accounting Office. In many cases, that's because a large chunk of savings was drained by the husband's medical bills.

FIGURE I.1 NUMBER OF U.S. WIDOWS BY AGE

AGE OF WIDOWS IN U.S.	NUMBER OF WIDOWS IN U.S.
Under 25 to 35	90,000
35 to 45	302,000
45 to 55	648,000
55 to 65	1,594,000
65 to 75	3,607,000
75 to 85	3,548,000
85 and up	1,424,000

Source: U.S. Census 1993.

- In 1993, there were 11.2 million widows in this country, according to the U.S. Bureau of the Census. (See Figure I.1.)

- The average age for a woman to be widowed in the United States is 55.

For every suddenly single woman, there's a different set of circumstances to navigate. No one else is going to have the same situation as yours. Here are some real-life examples of women who found themselves unexpectedly in the position of dealing with their own finances and their reactions. (To protect their privacy, last names are deleted.)

$

Melissa and James began dating in high school as first loves. As soon as they graduated from college, they married. While he studied for his doctorate, she supported both of them on her teaching salary. After completing school, James had excellent prospects. Employers from around the country were vying for his talents, and the money was good. With their two children ages 6 and 8, the couple moved from their hometown in Ohio to Connecticut so James could work at a leading pharmaceutical firm. Two years later, Melissa discovered her husband was having an affair with a woman he had met at a scientific conference. When she confronted him, he asked for a divorce. Melissa was shocked, bitter, and completely unprepared. She and James had been partners for more than 20 years; now, at age 40, she was alone, far from her family, and had two small children to raise on a modest teaching salary. James claimed he had no assets and was saddled with huge credit card debts. "He was finally starting to make some money, and I was planning to take some time off to spend with the kids," says Melissa. "Now I've got to fight him just to get child support. It's not fair."

$

Susan's husband, Craig, died of kidney cancer. At age 36, she was left to raise their children, ages 3 and 5. She had no job and no credit in her own name. Although her husband had been sick for three years, she was so wrapped up in caring for him that she never thought about how she'd manage without him. All of a sudden she had $115,000 in life insurance money and didn't know what to do with it. Wisely, she put her money in a money market account and signed up for a financial planning course at a community college. "I'm not sitting pretty, but I'm on my way to meeting my financial goals," says Susan.

$

Claire divorced her first husband after 13 years, when their children were ages 6 and 3. At the time, she was the breadwinner, bringing in $120,000 from her landscaping business. Her ex, who was unemployed, got the house in the divorce proceedings. Then her business went bust, and she was left with nothing. She started another business painting T-shirts and crafting jewelry as a way to scrape by. Four years later, she remarried a successful investment banker who encouraged her to quit work. A few months later, he died of a heart attack without a will. She quickly returned to work to keep the household solvent, but it was a struggle she will never forget. "Even with my business background, I hadn't taken the time to find out where any of the financial papers were kept," says Claire. In the end, she was unable to recover thousands of dollars invested with out-of-state brokerages.

$

Judy had lived off her wealthy father's income for her entire life. Sure, she had married and borne two children, but when the marriage collapsed, she went back to living off good old Dad. "I didn't want to think about anything having to do with money, except spending it," says Judy. Then her father died. She was 37, and her daughters were teenagers. Judy was completely ignorant about money matters and couldn't even find his bank accounts. "It was a mess," she recalls.

When she finally located all his papers, she found that her father had cashed in his life insurance policy, gambled away his fortune, and was, in fact, in substantial debt. A few months later, her mother and sister were killed in a plane crash, and she received a $50,000 insurance settlement. She hired her friend's brother, a broker, to invest the lump sum for her, thinking she could quickly make enough to live on. But the investment went south, fast. She lost everything. "I went from being an heiress with a maid and a house on the beach to having nothing," says Judy.

Chances are you will relate to some aspects of these women's stories. For each one, the transition to life alone was swift and painful, but each woman succeeded though tenacity and hard work. None of them found the change to be an easy one, but they are moving forward with their lives. Your decision to buy this book is your first step to rebuilding your financial life. Here's to managing your money solo. Good luck.

SUDDENLY SINGLE

CHAPTER ONE

$

Getting It Together

Not knowing what you actually have can cost you. Remarkably, it's not unusual, even if you are a professional woman, to have absolutely no notion of what insurance policies you and your husband have or what brokerage accounts or other investments you two have accumulated over the years. Such ignorance carries with it a high price. In a divorce, it might allow your ex to waltz away with assets you never even knew were rightfully yours. And if your spouse has died, it can leave you without access to cash from life insurance policies, pension plans, and other benefits for months or longer, depending on how much time it takes you to find the documents.

If you are fortunate, your husband and you keep all your important papers in some orderly fashion in a safe-deposit box or a file drawer. But most of us are simply not financially organized. We give lip service to our desire to neatly track our financial life, but frequently it's more talk than action. We toss monthly bills in one file, brokerage statements in another, and pension updates in yet another. Some documents we may keep in our offices, others in bank safe-deposit boxes or home offices. Your attorney may hold copies of your wills in his or her office, for instance. You may have absolutely no idea where some items are—say, your marriage certificate or husband's birth certificate.

In the weeks following your husband's death or the finalization of your divorce, you will be forced to make dozens of decisions about both your personal and your financial life. So it's critical to know what you have to work with. For widowed women, this can be an especially difficult interval if your husband was sick for a period of time, causing you to focus on doctors, hospitals, and his fight for his life rather than on money issues. Everything but the life-and-death struggle was likely put on hold.

Getting your finances in order straightaway might seem like a dreaded task, but it will make life easier. Women who are separated but not yet divorced will want to pull this material together as quickly as possible, *before* the divorce proceedings. It is vital information for your attorney to have in order for you to get the best settlement possible. Believe it or not, while everything else in your life seems to be out of control, this is one area you *can* control. You just have to get organized. And that means locating all the important financial documents.

To find out what assets you have to work with, you might need to do some detective work, but push yourself to get going. Managing money involves knowing what you have—everything from your bank accounts to brokerage accounts to retirement plans—and keeping an orderly system of paperwork.

For safekeeping, you should place all important documents in one big folder and store it in a locked file drawer or secure place that is easy to access. Be sure to keep the materials updated regularly.

HERE ARE THE PAPERS YOU WILL NEED TO LOCATE

- Copies of your joint tax returns for the past five years
- Records of both your husband's and your retirement accounts
- All insurance policies, including homeowner's, auto, health, life, and disability
- Current statements for all bank and brokerage accounts
- Current statements of mutual fund holdings
- The deed to your home or your domicile lease agreement
- Any business partnership agreements
- Birth certificates
- Marriage certificate
- List of credit cards and the names under which they are listed
- Title to your vehicle, car loan information, or lease agreements
- Most recent mortgage statement
- Employer stock option plans
- Wills, living wills
- Powers of attorney
- Receipts for major purchases
- Warranties
- Prenuptial or postnuptial agreements

WHAT ARE YOUR SOURCES OF MONEY?

Now that you have all your documents assembled in one place you can begin to get a feel for your financial picture. You may not understand exactly what it all means, but just gathering up the paperwork will take you a long way toward getting it all together. In essence, these documents represent a snapshot of your total assets. And that is what you are going to have to work with in the days and weeks ahead. These are your tools, so to speak. In later chapters, we will discuss how you will use this information to move ahead. For example, you'll need this material to establish a budget, figure out your net worth, and develop a financial plan. This is the only way you can accurately determine your financial situation.

You might have trouble locating some of these vital documents. Relax. What you need to do is think about who might have a record on hand. For example, your husband's insurance agent is sure to have a copy of his policy in his files. His employer will have records of his pension plans, his attorney will have the will, and so on. The following list represents the kinds of assets you can expect to find outlined in those important papers. Of course, not all of these sources of money will be available to you. Someone who has a defined benefit plan is probably not going to have a 401(k), for instance. If your husband is under age 30, chances are there won't be much in the way of life insurance benefits. Then, too, he may have invested only in mutual funds but no individual stocks.

RETIREMENT ASSETS

Annuity: This is a type of investment in which you or your husband, as policyholders, make payments to an insurance company. The money grows tax-free until you withdraw it at retirement. It earns interest and assures you a steady income as long as you live, or for a set time frame.

Defined benefit plan: This is a traditional pension plan in which an employer uses a formula based on salary and years of employment with the firm to devise an income to be paid to the employee or beneficiary on a regular basis at retirement.

401(k) plan: A retirement plan in which the employee makes regular, tax-deferred contributions from a salary each pay period. Often, the employer matches a percentage of the contribution. The employee then selects from a menu of investment choices, typically five, into which the funds are divided. *Vesting* is the employee's right to receive the employer-contributed funds after a set number of years of employment.

403(b) plan: Similar to a 401(k), these plans are offered to public employees and people who work for nonprofit organizations.

Individual Retirement Account (IRA): A tax-deferred pension plan that allows many people to invest up to $2,000 annually. Contributions are typically tax-deductible. The account is tax-free until you withdraw the money at retirement. Usually there is a penalty for removing the funds before age 59½, and you must start withdrawing the money at age 70½. A new type of IRA, the Roth IRA, is available beginning in 1998. It has a different set of rules and is free from federal tax when you withdraw the money.

Keogh plan: A tax-deferred retirement plan for the self-employed that lets a worker set aside up to 25% of income.

SEP-IRA: A retirement plan for someone who is self-employed. An IRA is opened and up to 13% of net earnings can be contributed, tax deferred until retirement.

Social Security: These are retirement funds paid by the federal government provided the person has been employed for at least 40 quarters.

Veterans benefits: These are funds paid by the federal government through the Veterans Administration to individuals who served in the U.S. Military.

INSURANCE POLICIES

Cash value life insurance: Policies such as whole life, variable life, and universal life that are a combination life insurance policy and investment savings plan.

Term life insurance: For a specified period, an annual premium provides a death benefit to survivors.

INVESTMENTS

Bonds: This is a debt of a corporation or the government. A bond buyer provides money to the institution, and it in turns pays back the sum with interest at a specified time.

Mutual funds: A selection of stocks and bonds or a mixture of investments that are pooled together, sold as shares to individual investors, and managed by a professional money manager.

Stocks: These are shares in a company that are sold to raise capital. There are more than 8,000 publicly traded companies.

BANK ACCOUNTS

Certificate of deposit (CD): An insured bank deposit with a guaranteed interest rate that is held for a set time period, usually three months, six months, one year, or five years.

Checking: A federally insured bank deposit that typically pays a low interest rate, but does not require any set time period before the funds are available. Payments to others are direct via paper checks or electronic means.

Money market: A federally insured bank account that typically pays higher interest than a regular savings account and requires a minimum investment.

Savings: A federally insured bank account that pays a higher rate of interest than a checking account and is liquid, but there are no check-writing capabilities.

OTHER ASSETS

Proceeds from real estate sales: The net amount received from the sale of a home, vacation house, or other property.

Proceeds from the sale of a business: The amount of money you may receive should a privately held business ownership be sold.

MAKE ROOM TO WORK

The next step is to set up an area in your home that you can use to work on the materials at hand. Some women just lay it all out on the dining room table and sort through the various files as needed. This will take time, so be prepared to forgo the use of that piece of furniture for months or even a year or more. Others use one room of the house as a base of financial operations. Everything is stored there, and copies of all correspondence are kept on file.

Next, try to schedule a certain chunk of time each day to devote to the task at hand, and stick to it. Accomplishing even one task per day will give you some semblance of order and get the process under way. Action is empowering, even if it only entails making a single phone call or sending one letter.

Once you've assembled all the papers and developed a filing system that makes it easy to find information on an as-needed basis, it's time to take stock of advisors and friends who might help you make sense of it all.

WHO CAN YOU TURN TO FOR FINANCIAL GUIDANCE?

Your husband may very well have been the provider in the house, paying the bills, keeping track of investment portfolios, and the like, but more often than not these days, women play a pivotal role in such day-to-day decisions. In part, that's because more of us are working full-time and contributing to the mutual pot. About 57.5 million women are now working, 42 million of them full-time. That's 56% of the adult female population, compared with just 32% in 1950. This means we need to know something about our money in order to make choices about our 401(k) plans and trim our income taxes, among other things.

Moreover, money has begun to lose its "macho" image, and it's no longer considered unfeminine to be knowledgeable about money and investing. Then, too, as we marry later in life, many of us long ago abandoned the outdated notion that a knight in shining armor would take care of us for the rest of our lives and we'd never have to worry our pretty little heads about money. We began to accept responsibility for our money lives and started saving and investing in our 20s rather than waiting for a man to do it for us as many of our mothers did.

It's quite possible you have even been the *primary* money manager, handling the household finances and making all the investment decisions. Women are now the primary money decision makers in 32% of the households that own mutual funds, up from 19% in 1992, according to a 1996 study conducted by the Investment Company Institute, the mutual fund trade association. Or maybe you and your husband shared the duties.

That financial knowledge will certainly serve you well in the future. But if you're like most women, financially competent or not, when your husband has died unexpectedly or your marriage has collapsed, you're going to have a hard time focusing on your money matters without some professional guidance. For Marty, age 43, whose husband was murdered, one of the most difficult adjustments was learning to make financial decisions on her own. "We always made the big decisions together," she says. "I wrote the checks, but he dealt with the insurance agent, our banker, and our accountant. I had never even done income taxes before. That blew me away," she recalls.

This might be a good time to make a list of the professionals you might need to contact for advice and help in sorting out your sources of income and putting together an investment strategy. You'll want to include their addresses and phone and fax numbers. To start assembling your future advisors, you should ask yourself who has helped you and your husband deal with your money matters in the past.

- Do you have a stockbroker you use regularly? Do you trust the person and feel comfortable continuing to invest with him or her, or will you need to find a new one?
- Do you have a financial planner?
- Do you have an attorney who will have your interests as a priority? This is critical for divorcées.
- Is there a personal banker or a trust officer who handles your accounts?
- What about an insurance agent?
- Who can give you the information you need about your husband's employee pension plan?

YOUR MONEY MAKEUP

While you are in the questioning mode, take a few minutes to sketch out your overall attitude about money. Before you start to actively manage your assets, you should have some inner understanding about how you relate to money, as well as your individual scenario at the present time and what it could be in the future. No two people have the same financial circumstances or handle money issues in the same way. As a result, we all have a different money profile.

Grab a notebook and write down your responses to the following 25 questions. This will help you get a better idea of your financial profile and will come in handy when you start making critical decisions about your money.

- What's your age?

- What is your biggest fear about money?

- What worries you most about your current money situation?

- Is your job secure?

- What's your current individual income?

- What are your financial goals? Do you want to be able to travel, keep your home, buy a new car?

- Are you a saver or a spender?

- Are you a conservative or an aggressive investor?

- If you had $1,000 to invest, would you put it in a guaranteed investment like a money market account or a CD, or would you invest it in a noninsured mutual fund that will rise and fall with the market?

- How important is it to you to spend money on material goods like clothes or vacations?

- What kind of lifestyle have you been living? Will you have to scale back?

- How difficult will that be for you?

- Will you inherit money one day? How much is it likely to be and how soon?

- Do you see yourself as a financially independent person or a dependent one?

- Are you a knowledgeable investor?

- Do you tend to take other peoples' advice about investing, or are you a do-it-yourselfer capable of conducting your own research?

- Do you know how to budget?

- What money role did you play in your relationship? Were you the bill payer, the investor, the budgeteer?

- What role did your husband play in your financial life?

- Do you have children to raise and educate?

- Can you support yourself and your children on your own income or financial resources?

- Are you an indulgent parent?

- Will you be able to spend less on your children and not feel guilty?

- Will you have to support your parents one day, or do you already?

- How many years until you retire?

While these questions cover a broad money landscape, your answers will let you begin to draw a unique portrait of yourself in relation to money. You'll definitely find this knowledge helpful as you begin to build your own financial life. In the next chapter, widows will learn which tasks must be handled at once and which phone calls and decisions can be postponed for a while.

It's important to learn this distinction because there are only so many hours in a day. Just because you're suddenly on your own doesn't mean the rest of the world has come to a screeching halt. You may very well be working a full-time job, running a household, and juggling countless other day-to-day activities that make demands on your time. Few of us can dedicate entire days to straightening out the paperwork and getting up to speed financially. No doubt "first things first" will take on a whole new meaning to you.

CHAPTER TWO

Actions for Widows

N o one ever wants to think about losing a partner. It's really impossible—both emotionally and financially—to be prepared when it happens. Even people who are the most forthright about money, financial planning, and investing dance around the discussion of death. The simple task of writing a will is problematic for many people. Simply put, for lots of us, facing mortality is downright disturbing. Who wants to think about it? Even a discussion about buying life insurance is somehow seen as morbid. It's not unusual for couples who have been married for years not to have a will or life insurance coverage, particularly if they are childless.

But when death does strike, the emotional and psychological blow can be devastating. Without some of these basic protections in place, your world can turn truly chaotic, whether you have children or not. Hopefully, you and your husband have taken the time to talk about what would happen when one of you dies. Perhaps you've even taken steps to prepare. You'll be in far better shape if you have. Too often, the most intense education of your life begins at a time when you are in a state of emotional distress.

It's normal to feel numb and out of control. There never seems to be enough time to prepare for this kind of life-shattering event. You're grieving. You're afraid. And you just want to be left alone, please. But there are several things that you simply must handle—soon. And truthfully, only you can make this happen. Some things are fine to put on hold until you have survived the initial shock and begun to adjust to your new lifestyle. For instance, there's no reason to uproot yourself from your home immediately, no rush to remarry, quit your job, or make any large investment decisions. It's important to know those areas on which you need to focus your full attention, and then just do it, one step at a time.

That said, however, you're going to feel pressure from friends, family, and financial advisors to make decisions. The pressure and unsolicited advice are probably very well intentioned, but you'll be better off if you stick to your own schedule. In the weeks after your spouse's death, you are going to be swamped with paperwork. You shouldn't feel that everything is falling on your head and that you need to decide everything now. Here's your priority to-do list.

ROUND 1: GETTING ORGANIZED

FIND EMOTIONAL SUPPORT

Find a grief counselor, therapist, or support group. No one can afford emotionally to be alone at this time. Your church or temple may be able to make recommendations for you. You'll never be able to tackle your finances until you have some kind of psychological and emotional support system in place. Once you have that to lean on, you can move into the actual tasks at hand.

OBTAIN DEATH CERTIFICATES

You'll need to make about two dozen copies of your husband's death certificate. You'll be required to send this document to everyone from credit card companies to the mortgage holder and his insurers to verify the death. It's best to make all these copies at once, then stick them in a file to send as needed.

NOTIFY THE DECEASED'S EMPLOYER

Notify your husband's employer and file for any benefits owed to you, such as pension income, life insurance payouts, and health insurance coverage. To do so, contact the person in charge of employee benefits; usually the human resource department can direct you. Your letter should state clearly your husband's full name and Social Security number, the date he died, and a request for information on widow's benefits.

Ask if there are any settlement options for you to consider. If your husband had pension benefits, you may have a choice between lump-sum or lifetime payments. Be sure to provide a phone number where you can be reached if there are any questions.

You may need to contact more than one employer if your husband qualified for more than one plan. Other retirement plans such as IRAs or Keoghs should be notified as well. If you were named *beneficiary* (that is, the person designated to receive the proceeds) these assets can be invested in your own tax-deferred account. You should also change the beneficiary on any of your own retirement accounts if your husband had previously been named.

FILE INSURANCE CLAIMS

File a claim with your husband's life insurance company.

Your husband's insurance agent should have applicable policy information and can help you get the necessary forms.

Or you can send a letter to the insurance company, including a copy of the death certificate and your husband's policy number, requesting the forms necessary to file a claim. You can choose to receive the money as a lump payment or in installments over a certain period.

CONTACT GOVERNMENT OFFICES

Contact your state's office for inheritance tax.

Change the title and registration of any cars or trucks listed in your husband's name by contacting your local department of motor vehicles. You'll want the registration in your name when you sell the car.

The Social Security Administration (800-772-1213) will need to be notified. You can apply by phone or go to a local office to sign a claim form. You must have been married for at least nine months prior to your spouse's death to be eligible for benefits. However, if death is a result of an accident or military duty, no minimum length of marriage is required. You can also qualify if your spouse is the parent of your child—natural or adopted. You will need both your husband's and your birth certificates, your Social Security numbers, and your marriage certificate. If you have children who are still dependent, you'll also need their birth certificates and Social Security numbers. You must also produce your husband's W-2 forms for the past two years if he was still working at the time of his death.

If you feel up to it, you might want to check on your own Social Security benefits at the same time to be sure your benefits are accruing properly. You can request a copy of your Earnings and Benefit Estimate Statement (see Figure 2.1) from the Social Security Administration free of charge when you call their toll-free number. You can fix any mistakes and be sure they have accurate data about your earnings history.

FIGURE 2.1 EARNINGS AND BENEFIT ESTIMATE

This form furnished courtesy of WILLIAM MERCER

Form Approved
OMB No. 0960-0466

☐ SP

Request for Earnings and Benefit Estimate Statement

☐ Please check this box if you want to get your statement in Spanish instead of English.

Please print or type your answers. When you have completed the form, fold it and mail it to us.

1. Name shown on your Social Security card:

First Name _____ Middle Initial _____

Last Name Only _____

2. Your Social Security number as shown on your card:

☐☐☐ – ☐☐ – ☐☐☐☐

3. Your date of birth
   Month — Day — Year

4. Other Social Security numbers you have used:
   ☐☐☐ – ☐☐ – ☐☐☐☐
   ☐☐☐ – ☐☐ – ☐☐☐☐

5. Your sex: ☐ Male ☐ Female

6. Other names you have used
   (including a maiden name):
   _____

Form SSA-7004-SM (SPEC) (4-95) Destroy prior editions

For items 7 and 9 show only earnings covered by Social Security. Do NOT include wages from State, local or Federal Government employment that are NOT covered for Social Security or that are covered ONLY by Medicare.

7. Show your actual earnings (wages and/or net self-employment income) for last year and your estimated earnings for this year:

   A. Last year's actual earnings: *(Dollars Only)*

   $ ☐☐☐ , ☐☐☐ . 0 0

   B. This year's estimated earnings: *(Dollars Only)*

   $ ☐☐☐ , ☐☐☐ . 0 0

8. Show the age at which you plan to stop working.

   ☐☐ *(Show only one age)*

9. Below, show the average yearly amount (not your total future lifetime earnings) that you think you will earn between now and when you plan to stop working. Include cost-of-living, performance or scheduled pay increases or bonuses.

   If you expect to earn significantly more or less in the future due to promotions, job changes, part-time work, or an absence from the work force, enter the amount that most closely reflects your future average yearly earnings.

   If you don't expect any significant changes, show the same amount you are earning now (the amount in 7B).

   Future average yearly earnings: *(Dollars Only)*

   $ ☐☐☐ , ☐☐☐ . 0 0

---

10. Address where you want us to send the statement.

Name _____

Street Address (Include Apt. No., P.O. Box, or Rural Route) _____

City _____ State _____ Zip Code _____

Notice:
I am asking for information about my own Social Security record or the record of a person I am authorized to represent. I understand that when requesting information on a deceased person, I must include proof of death and relationship or appointment. I further understand that if I deliberately request information under false pretenses , I may be guilty of a Federal crime and could be fined and/or imprisoned. I authorize you to use a contractor to send the statement of earnings and benefit estimates to the person named in item 10.

▲

Please sign your name (Do Not Print)

_____

Date _____ (Area Code) Daytime Telephone No. _____

17

The longer you wait after you turn 65 to tap into your husband's Social Security funds, the higher will be the amount of the payments. You might not be able to afford to wait, though. Under current rules, if you are at least 60, but under age 65, you can claim benefits. If you are not yet 60, but have kids under the age of 16 living with you, you may also claim benefits. If you are under age 60, with no dependents, you can still apply for the funeral expense reimbursement of $255 today.

If your husband was a veteran, contact the Department of Veterans Affairs. They offer a toll-free number in all states. You may be eligible for a pension of some sort. They will also pay some funeral and burial expenses. You will, however, probably need a record of his military discharge papers.

CONTACT FINANCIAL SERVICES PROVIDERS

Meet with your bank manager. If your husband had an account in his name alone, it should be changed to an account called "Estate of." You'll need your spouse's Social Security number to secure an estate tax ID number, which you can then use as the account number. Deposit all income from your husband's assets under the new number, and pay any estate administration expenses (such as the funeral cost) from this account. Any joint accounts should be transferred to an account in your name. You'll need a copy of the death certificate to do so. As for outstanding checks, you can decide to honor them or not. Then, too, you might be able to renegotiate the terms of any outstanding loans with your banker.

Contact your stockbroker and ask for the necessary paperwork to change the accounts to either your name or the estate's account. To change the name on a joint account, you'll need to show a copy of the death certificate, an affidavit of domicile (the stockbroker has this), and a letter of request with your Social Security number. Ask your broker to give you a value on the assets in your husband's accounts and your joint accounts at the time of his death. Your estate taxes will be based on that valuation.

PAY YOUR BILLS

Whatever you do pay your bills. Sure it's easy to stuff them in an envelope and deal with them later, long after the funeral and estate issues have been settled. But you'll live to regret that decision, and it will cost you far more than an unending stream of irritating bill-collector calls. Creditors aren't so softhearted these days that they will give you a bereavement grace period. Failure to make your monthly payments can result in onerous interest charges, late fees, and a tarnished credit record that can haunt you for years.

So clear off a work space, pull out a clean financial ledger, and divide up your bills, your husband's bills, and your joint debts. Then note the debtor, the total amount owed, and the minimum payment required. You'll need to pay as many of these as you can in a timely fashion. You'll want to pay your bills and the joint bills, if possible. His bills should be handled by his estate.

But scrutinize every bill carefully to be sure it is legit. Be sharp-eyed, and don't pay any bill that looks unfamiliar. Ask for verification from the creditor if the bill doesn't look right to you. As lousy as it may sound, this is a time when all sorts of unscrupulous types surface in hopes of getting some free pickings.

Anne's husband, for instance, bought a Ferrari with cash three weeks before he committed suicide. About six months after the funeral, the dealer who sold him the car contacted Anne and told her that the car had never been paid for and he was going to have to repossess it if she didn't pay up. For-

TAX TIPS

- Your husband's estate is not subject to *estate taxes* (taxes levied on a deceased's assets) if the net worth is less than $625,000 (this sum will increase each year till it reaches $1 million in 2006). Anything above that is subject to a tax and is due nine months after the date of his death. It is paid by the estate, though, not by you directly.

- The estate consists of your husband's ownership portion of any real estate holdings, including your home, investments, automobiles, boats, retirement benefits, business interests, and life insurance death benefit.

- You can avoid estate tax altogether if your husband has left everything to you (providing you are a U.S. citizen). Under the unlimited marital deduction, any assets you inherit directly from your spouse, such as life insurance benefits, certificates of deposit, or bank accounts, are not subject to federal income tax.

- There is a *unified credit* of $192,800, which can nicely offset any estate taxes on the first $600,000 of property transfers. The exemption increases until it reaches $1 million in 2006.

- When you inherit a home or investments such as stocks and bonds, you pay tax only when you sell and only on the growth after you inherited it.

- An annual tax return must be filed for the earnings and investment income that your husband accumulated up to the date he died. The return for that year must be filed with the Internal Revenue Service by April 15 of the following year. Usually, the executor of the estate is responsible for filing it; if not, you are responsible for filing. The form is the same as if your husband were still living, but "deceased" must be typed after his name, along with the date of death.

- You may file a joint tax return for the year in which your spouse dies and pay under that tax rate. On the line where you sign the return, you must indicate in writing that you are filing as a surviving spouse. The following year, you may file as either a single taxpayer or a surviving spouse. The tax tables for each differ.

- For a refund, you'll need to file a separate form, called Form 1310, Statement of a Person Claiming Refund Due a Deceased Taxpayer.

- You should deduct all the medical bills incurred by your husband during the year in which he died, even if you don't pay them until up to 12 months later.

tunately, after some frantic searching, she found a receipt, and the dealer quit hassling her.

ROUND 2: UPDATE YOUR INSURANCE

After you've made it through that first rigorous to-do list, give yourself a well-deserved break, and then gear up for the next set of money matters. These steps should be handled before too much time passes, although not necessarily in the first few weeks.

UPDATE YOUR HEALTH INSURANCE COVERAGE

If your spouse worked for a company that has a health plan covering 20 or more employees, under the terms of the Consolidated Omnibus Reconciliation Act, or *COBRA,* a federal law, the plan must continue to offer you and any dependents coverage for at least 18 months and can usually be stretched up to three years if you have dependent children. You will be responsible for paying the premiums, though. You have 60 days to decide to stick with your spouse's plan.

If this is not an option, you might be able to switch to your own employer's plan, if there is one, or sign up for a group policy though your union, an association, or a religious group that you belong to. If you are a real estate agent, for example, contact the local trade association.

Should you strike out, you'll have to buy your own health insurance policy. Unfortunately, individual policies are not cheap. The goal is to find a comprehensive policy that will cover a minimum of 80% of your medical and hospital bills once you meet the *deductible* (amount you pay before the insurer picks up the tab, usually $100 to $200 a year for an individual or close to $600 for a family policy). The remaining 20% will come out of your pocket.

Shop for a policy that caps your yearly out-of-pocket copayments at $1,000 to $2,000. Make sure the policy has a lifetime minimum coverage of at least $1 million and is guaranteed to be renewable. That way the insurer can't jack up your rates or cancel the policy altogether if you fall ill. Of course, you can expect rates to rise over the years. Look for good-health or nonsmoker discounts, too. And make a point of reading the policy's restrictions carefully—some exclude or limit coverage for preexisting conditions like diabetes or multiple sclerosis.

To find an affordable policy, you might want to call your state Blue Cross/Blue Shield plan, the largest fee-for-service insurers in the country. You can also call your state insurance department to find out about any HMOs or other managed care plans in your area that offer individual policies. Or check with your doctor or a local hospital. Only about a quarter of HMOs offer plans for individuals. Your state's insurance department can also help you track down a policy, even if you have some health problems that make it tough to get insurance. These are called *high-risk policies.*

Here are two other sources that can help you find a policy and compare rates of various insurers:

USAA, 800-531-8000, sells directly to individuals.

Quotesmith, 800-556-9393, searches a database and sends a list of choices free of charge.

UPDATE YOUR DISABILITY INSURANCE

You might already have some *disability insurance* (which pays benefits if you are unable to work) from your employer, but it probably isn't going to be enough. Most employer plans cover just 60% of your annual income. In fact, only about one-third of big U.S. employers provide any coverage at all. Some states, including New York and California, require employers to offer short-term disability insurance that might last up to six months.

But without the benefit of a second income to fall back on if something happens to you either physically or emotionally to prevent you from working, you'll need to boost that coverage. Claire, for instance, went back to work 10 days after her husband's death. Six months later, she fell into deep depression and was out of work for seven weeks.

For a policy that will replace 60% of your income, expect to pay at least $1,000 a year in premiums, or about 2% of your salary. You can lower that amount by opting for a longer waiting period (say, 30 to 90 days) before benefits kick in.

REVIEW YOUR LIFE INSURANCE

Life insurance should be taken care of in a speedy fashion only if you have dependents. If you're widowed with dependent kids, you might want to buy extra insurance since you are now your children's only means of support. If you are a single mother, ask yourself how long your children will need your financial support. How much life insurance you need depends on how many children you have and how old they are. One guideline suggested by financial planners is to buy coverage worth about 8 to 10 times your annual salary.

Term insurance is the simplest and most affordable life insurance to buy if you plan to insure yourself for at least 20 years. You pay an annual premium based on your age, your health, the cost of paying the agent's commission, and how much the insurer thinks it can earn by investing your premium until you die. If you are age 45 and in good health, a 15-year policy for $100,000 might cost you $250 a year in premiums. Term insurance pays a specific death benefit to your survivors.

The other form of life insurance, called *cash value insurance,* is a combination of a life policy and a savings plan. There are several types of these policies. The most common are whole life, universal life, and variable life. *Whole life* invests your money mostly in bonds, and you get a fixed return and a traditional death benefit. *Universal life* lets you decide how much you want to pay in premiums and sets the death benefit accordingly. Universal life, unlike whole life, offers a variable interest rate that depends on the current market rate. The amount of your funds that exceeds the annual premium cost is invested for you and is tax deferred. *Variable life* invests money in a choice of stocks, bonds, and money market funds. The growth is tax deferred. A portion of the money pays for your annual premiums. You can withdraw the money when you retire. Women who make more than $100,000 and want around $700,000 in coverage might shop for a cash policy.

One of the best places to find a policy is with a discount broker who sells low-load insurance without going through an agent. The commission can be as much as 50% cheaper. Low-load policies pay an average return of 6.7% after five years. The average commission-based policy, on the other hand, has a negative return after 5 years and takes at least 15 years to start producing decent returns.

Keep in mind, though, if you cash in your policy during the first couple of years you will lose all of your investment. Typically, it takes five years for cash value policyholders to see any returns. (See Figure 2.2.) The Consumer Federation of America advises that you steer clear of such a policy unless you can hang onto it for at least 20 years. That lets the cash value portion of the policy build up. About one-quarter of policyholders, however, stop paying into them after three years.

The rates of return on cash life insurance policies vary widely from year to year and from policy to policy. The policies are terribly complex, and many agents are unable to explain them properly to consumers. But you can have specific cash value policies analyzed by using CFA's Life Insurance Rate of Return Analysis Service, which estimates true investment returns on any cash value life insurance policy illustration. Call CFA at 202-387-0087 for more information about this service, which costs $40 for the first illustration.

- Check out insurance firms, like USAA Life (800-531-8000) or Ameritas (800-552-3553), that sell policies directly to you without going through an agent.

- To get the best-priced policy, you might ask a quote service company to send you the five best-priced policies that suit your needs. Most don't charge for the service, and you can buy the policy from them.

  Insurance Quote Services Inc., 800-972-1104

  SelectQuote, 800-343-1985

  TermQuote, 800-444-8376

  Quotesmith Corp., 800-556-9393

- Be sure to check the individual insurer's credit ratings. Independent evaluators include A.M. Best (908-439-2200),

FIGURE 2.2 AVERAGE ANNUAL RATES OF RETURN ON LIFE INSURANCE POLICIES

YEAR	RATE OF RETURN (PERCENT)
1	−87.9
2	−54.9
3	−18.9
4	0.0
5	5.6
6	7.3
7	7.7
8	7.7
9	7.6
10	9.8
11	8.0
12	8.0
13	8.0
14	7.9
15	8.1
16	7.8
17	7.8
18	7.8
19	7.8

Source: Consumer Federation of America

Standard & Poor's (212-208-1527), and Weiss Group (800-289-9222).

- Look for reputable designations like *Chartered Financial Consultant* (ChFC) and *Charted Life Underwriter* (CLU), both awarded by the American College in Bryn Mawr, Pennsylvania, the insurance and financial industry's stellar institution of higher learning.

- Even though all you want to do is shut out the world and give yourself time to cope with your loss, getting professional advice from early on will make your financial future more manageable.

PUT YOUR MONEY SOMEPLACE SAFE

Keep in mind that you are not looking to hook up with some stock jockey. The goal is to find someone you feel comfortable with who can help you get your finances in order and start you on the road to educating yourself about money.

You'll want to set up appointments with your attorney and accountant if you have them. A financial planner is another good resource for some advice on how to invest any insurance payout. If you don't already have one, you might want to check around with some friends or relatives to see if they have any good recommendations. You can also call the National Association of Personal Financial Advisors (800-366-2732) for a list of fee-only advisors in your town. Or check with the American Institute of Certified Public Accountants in New York for a list of *Personal Financial Specialists* (their approved financial planning accountants) (212-318-0500).

Keep in mind, though, this is a time for short-term decisions. Most financial planners suggest you refrain from investing any lump-sum insurance or pension payout for at least six months, and ideally, a year. The best place to stash money is in liquid money market funds, short-term certificates of deposit or Treasury bills.

Then, too, there are an increasing number of "branchless" banks that do business by phone, mail, and on the World Wide Web and offer yields well above the national average. Because they don't have the overhead that banks with branches have, they can pass along their savings by paying higher interest rates. Many of the branchless banks aren't traditional banks at all. Credit card issuers and Internet-only financial companies are among the most aggressive rate setters.

Like any bank, those without branches offer CDs and money market accounts that are federally insured. Minimum investments range from $100 to $5,000, which must be deposited by mail with an application. (Subsequent investments can be made by electronic transfer.) The rate you are quoted is typically good for seven days. While these accounts are probably too conservative for the long term, they provide a good place to invest your money while you get your act together.

Here are some institutions offering top CD and money market yields:

American Express, 800-297-8800

Atlanta Internet Bank, http://www.atlantabank.com or 888-256-6932

1st Source Bank, http://www.1stsource.com

MBNA America, 800-577-3556

TeleBank, 800-638-2265

WHAT NOT TO DO

In short, you'll be getting advice from all directions. *The biggest mistake newly widowed women make is to listen to hot invest-*

ment tips or advice from well-meaning family members or friends. Sure you're worried about whether you have enough money to make ends meet, and the promise of a surefire investment is hard to resist. But you're a prime target for unscrupulous salespeople from all sorts of investment outfits touting investments that "guarantee" returns of 15% or more. These people scan the local newspapers for obituaries and then ring you up with a pitch for some slick investment. That kind of tip is usually just too good to be true. Well-intentioned relatives and friends, too, tend to want to offer you advice that has worked for them, but it may be off base for you.

So pass on it for now. Wait until you have a stronger understanding of money management or until your head has cleared before you even consider checking out such investments. While it's probably true that you'd prefer to have someone else make financial decisions for you to help you build financial security, sit tight. The time will come when you can begin to take action and develop your master plan.

You probably shouldn't move from your home immediately, but as time goes by you might want to consider it to cut costs. Initially, hanging on to your home can be comforting. But eventually the upkeep can dig into any kind of fixed-income principal you're depending on, and the taxes and other home-related expenses, such as lawn care, can really bust your budget.

There's no rush to switch your utility and telephone accounts to your name. Keeping the phone in your husband's name for a time can ward off those unwanted salespeople who prey on widows. Credit card companies should be notified, but this can wait until you have established credit in your own name by getting your own credit card, if you haven't already done so. Eventually, you will want to notify all clubs, alumni groups, and other organizations you and your husband belong to. Some clubs may let you retain a membership at reduced dues.

In the next chapter, we'll discuss what you need to do at once if you think your marriage is in jeopardy, or if you are separated, and what can wait. Some of the advice is not so different from what widows need to do, but the approach is quite different and the obstacles a bit trickier to navigate since this is about dividing assets. But if you are confident, you'll get through it with a minimal amount of emotional and financial scarring.

CHAPTER THREE

$

Things to Do if Your Marriage Is in Jeopardy

Oftentimes, women whose husbands die have little warning or time to prepare to take charge of their financial affairs. But if your marriage is heading for divorce, you *can* get your act together ahead of time. You just have to make the right moves early on. For most of you, the biggest problem is going to be a psychological one—overcoming denial.

If you're like Melissa, whose husband left her for another woman, you probably think you can win your husband back. You convince yourself that this is just a temporary situation and cling to the hope that everything will work out in time. You go to counseling sessions and pray that everything will return to normal. You delude yourself into thinking that a few months of separation will give him time to have his fling and be done with it. Then, too, you fall for your husband's tale of financial troubles and don't fight for what's rightfully yours. Empathy will get you nowhere.

Of course, it's not that you're simply naive. This reaction is perfectly natural. You want to believe the person you've spent years of your life living with, side by side, day by day, wouldn't really want to harm you. Down deep there's a layer of trust that makes you unable to fathom that the marriage is over or that your husband would deny you and your kids the support you deserve.

So you do nothing but wait and worry and feel rejected and lousy about yourself and, understandably, angry with your spouse. But worst of all, you refuse to deal with the key money issues; you freeze. You must get it together and stare it square in the face. Once the love is gone, money is *the* issue, the *only* issue. It's what will help you live through the upheaval and start over. You must be coldhearted. Maybe that's not attractive, but it's survival at this point.

Of course, that initial separation doesn't mean your marriage is over. Reconciliation is always possible. But the fact is, your spouse might decide not to try to get the marriage back on track, period. Then again, he might want to come back, sheepishly begging for forgiveness, but *you've* already tossed in the towel and moved on with your life.

The fact is that 4 out of 10 marriages today end in divorce. While that's down from 50% a decade ago, it is still usually the wife who loses out financially. When couples split, the wife's standard of living plummets by around 30% in the first year after a divorce, while the husband's rises 10% or more. Untangling your personal life from that of your husband is going to be wrenching. Untangling your finances from those of your soon-to-be ex-spouse is superdifficult.

And don't count on alimony from your darling hubbie to bail you out while you struggle for financial independence. Alimony, once a standard "gift" from an ex, has become a relic of the past. Fewer than 15% of divorced women are awarded it. Even if you were to have the option, it typically lasts just a handful of years. In some states, alimony is provided only if the marriage lasted at least 10 years. Accepting a lump sum of money as part of a divorce settlement is probably better than agreeing to alimony payments anyway. It's a bird in hand, so to speak.

Here's what you need to do first if your marriage is on the verge of collapsing.

CALL AN ATTORNEY

Even if things are just starting to get rocky, you need to get some advice from an impartial outsider. These are highly emotional times, and a friend's advice just won't cut it now. This is a matrimonial battlefield, and you've got to look out for yourself. That's especially true if you have children. In 1993, for example, the poverty rate for children living with divorced mothers was nearly four times higher than for children in two-parent families.

Just going for a consultation doesn't mean you've set in motion a course that can't be reversed. It just makes good sense to hire someone who can help you evaluate your assets and press for the best-possible settlement. You need to know how long the divorce proceedings will take. Will it be a three-month operation or two years of back-and-forth exchanges? How much are you going to need to live on during that time?

Ask your recently divorced friends and colleagues or your tax or estate attorney for attorney recommendations. You want to be sure the attorney is someone who specializes in matrimonial law. Moreover, avoid using the same attorney your husband uses. It seems obvious, but often, especially when a divorce isn't a bitter one, couples opt to save money by having one lawyer do it all. Forget it. You want someone looking out for your best interests, not someone whose job is to make sure the divorce is pushed through smoothly and cheaply. If you are unfamiliar with the lawyer you have selected, you might want to check with your city and state attorney's office to make sure that person is in good standing, with no complaints lodged against him or her.

Use your lawyer's time wisely. When you are paying any-where from $200 to $600 an hour for legal counsel, you want concrete discussions about your *finances,* not about your emo-tional distress. See a therapist to help you deal with those per-sonal feelings. This negotiation is about cold cash.

DO-IT-YOURSELF DIVORCES

You might be able to skip attorney fees if you and your spouse have just a handful of assets, have been married a rel-atively short period of time, have no children, and have hardly any debt. These do-it-yourself divorces can be exe-cuted by calling your local divorce court and requesting the correct form. There are also several books available at local bookstores that deal with this specific approach to divorce.

MEDIATION

Mediation is also an option. Although the process differs from state to state, the idea is that you and your soon-to-be ex hire someone who is a professional divorce mediator to work out an agreement that is fair to both of you. The hourly sessions usually cost between $50 and $200 and might involve up to five sessions. You will need a lawyer to review the final agree-ment and file it in your local divorce court. Mediation works only if you know the total value of all your assets and where they are located. To find a mediator, check your local yellow pages under "divorce assistance."

LEARN THE THREE BASIC ELEMENTS OF DIVORCE

To fully take advantage of applicable laws, you should bone up on three important factors: alimony, child support, and division of property.

ALIMONY

Although it is quickly becoming a thing of the past, *alimony* is essentially the sum of money that an ex is legally required to pay under a separation agreement or a divorce decree. It is taxable income to you, not to him. If you have never worked outside the home, you will probably be entitled to some funds for a limited period of time, depending on how long you were married and the potential earning power of each partner.

CHILD SUPPORT

Every state has its own rules for figuring out the appropriate amount of *child support* for divorcing parents. Usually, child support payments last until the youngest child is 18, depending on your state. These payments are not taxable. You can get a copy of your state's support formula from your attorney or a clerk in the divorce court.

DIVISION OF PROPERTY IN YOUR STATE

Here are the three basic definitions.

Community property: All the property and assets accumulated during your marriage are considered to be community property, which is divided equally between the two divorcing parties. Property acquired before the marriage and inherited property are excluded. The community-property states are Arizona, California, Idaho, Louisiana, Nevada, New Mexico, Texas, Washington, and Wisconsin.

Common-law property: Property divided according to who holds the title to the asset is considered common-law property.

Equitable distribution: This is the basic method of distributing property in 40 states plus the District of Columbia. The court decides how to divide the assets based on criteria such as need, earnings potential, and financial contribution to the marriage. Keep in mind that *equitable* does not always mean *fair.*

ESTABLISH YOUR OWN CREDIT

It's critical to establish your own *credit record.* Before you make any sudden moves, you'll want to make certain that you have a credit card in your name alone. If you do not, apply for one immediately, before you agree to separate. Even in today's marriages, women who may have been supporting themselves for a decade or so before marrying buy into this idea of holding joint credit cards with their husbands.

Husbands frequently ask their new wives to cancel cards held prior to the marriage and carry jointly held plastic only. Their argument is that you should share everything. They are afraid you will somehow use this to hide your spending. Men see this as a trust issue, while women see it as one of control. Every woman needs a Visa or MasterCard in her own name. Department store cards and American Express don't have the same credit value as a Visa or MasterCard. It's important not only to have your own line of credit, but also to build a solid credit record by paying off the balance regularly and on time. A healthy credit history is worth its weight in gold at this stage in your life.

After you have your own credit in place, *close all joint credit card accounts.* Inform credit companies in writing that you want the accounts closed and will not be responsible for any charges from that time on. Request an accounting of outstanding charges. You can either pay them off yourself or make a deal with your ex. The balance must be paid off before they will close the account.

Notify all other creditors of your change in status if you are divorcing. This means contacting your mortgage holder, bank loan officer, and any other nonplastic creditor.

Your bank is the next stop. *If you don't already have checking and savings accounts in your name, open them.* Again, this notion of separating money in a marriage is usually pretty emotional. Men feel that if you want your own accounts you are not being a team player—a wrongheaded notion, but one that is very common. The thinking is that it is all "our" money. This can be a major mistake when you are in the throes of a divorce. You've got to separate your money quickly and cleanly. It just gets messy when it is all pooled together.

In general, women who are separated but not yet divorced should close any joint bank accounts. In some cases, though, you might want to keep the joint account open temporarily to pay for household expenses until the settlement is final. If that's the case, ask the bank to freeze the account. That way both your signature and his are required before any transaction can be made.

If you have any joint brokerage accounts, write at once and notify them that you are separated from your husband. Ask the broker not to make any transactions without your approval. If you have a *margin account* that lets you borrow money from the brokerage to make other investments, this step is critical. You don't want your husband investing with that borrowed money because you'll be liable not only for the loan, but the interest as well. That's especially troubling if the investment goes south.

DETERMINE YOUR NET WORTH

Find out just what you're worth. By putting a dollar amount on what you own (*assets*) and what you owe (*liabilities*), you can calculate your *net worth* (assets minus liabilities). You may think you know what your assets are, but don't assume so. Your husband may hold properties or investments about which you are clueless. You may not even have the correct information about his pension or pensions if he has worked for several employers over the course of his career. A hard-nosed assessment of your financial situation is crucial.

Even in the best of unions, it's a good idea to check up on how your partnership is faring financially on an annual basis. However, if you haven't done so and are heading for a separation, do so at once. Figure 3.1 is a worksheet that can help you figure out your assets as a couple. For pension sums, call your respective employers' benefits departments. This is all information that you are entitled to know, so be persistent.

You might not be able to get the precise value for all your assets, but do your best to track down an approximate value. Hire an appraiser if need be to get a realistic value on your furnishings, jewelry, and collectibles. Check out the contents of any safe-deposit box, and make sure you haven't missed any deeds or documents that will add to your list. Your tax return from last year will help identify any assets you may have forgotten to include. For those of you who are really having trouble gathering the numbers, you should call your accountant or insurance agent.

FIGURE 3.1 ASSETS

ASSET	$ AMOUNT
Cash in checking and savings accounts	
Certificates of deposit	
Money market account funds	
Bonds	
Mutual funds	

FIGURE 3.1   (CONTINUED)

ASSET	$ AMOUNT
Individual stocks	
Treasury bills	
401(k)s	
IRAs	
Pensions	
Profit-sharing plans	
Annuities	
Cash value insurance policies	
Your home	
Vacation house	
Rental property	
Antiques/furnishings	
Business equity	
Other property: boats, cars, horses, etc.	
TOTAL (assets)	

Now figure out what you and your husband owe to others by filling in the worksheet in Figure 3.2.

It's fairly easy to track down those to whom you owe money, but if there's a problem, call each credit card issuer, your mortgage holder, and other creditors to get an up-to-date accounting. For a list of creditors, you might want to contact one of the big three credit raters—Equifax (800-685-1111), Experian (800-682-7654), and Trans Union (800-888-4213). They can give you a copy of your credit report, which

FIGURE 3.2 LIABILITIES

YOUR DEBT	AMOUNT
Mortgage	
Home equity loan	
Other property loans	
Car loans	
College loans	
Credit card debt	
Other loans	
TOTAL (debts)	
Assets (from Figure 3.1)	
Less debts	
TOTAL (your household net worth)	

will list all your creditors. You might even turn up a credit card or two that your husband has been carrying without your knowledge. Once your divorce is final, inform the credit bureaus in writing of your new status and request that all of your credit data be listed in your name only.

INCOME AND BUDGETING

Now you'll want to take some time to ask yourself what your sources of income are. Will you need to find another job that pays more in order to support yourself? What can you afford to pay for living expenses such as rent or a mortgage? Will you need to ask your husband for financial support? Will he ask you for it? This is not as strange as it sounds. With women moving into higher-ranked corporate positions, their salaries have risen accordingly. Today, some woman earn as much or more than their husbands do. Then, too, you may have inherited money, and he may decide he wants a portion of that as well. Either way, knowing what you have coming in is essential to putting together a financial plan.

You'll want to establish a monthly budget early on that works for you. You should plan to set aside an emergency fund that will equal three to six months of living expenses. Devising a budget that will let you live within your means is essential. You'll probably have to cut back on spending until you get your finances on solid ground. We will discuss how to outline a budget in the next chapter.

UPDATE YOUR INSURANCE

Typical divorce settlements specify that the children are beneficiaries of your ex-spouse's life insurance. But you'll want to quickly change the beneficiary on your own current life insurance. It's essential to insure your life even if your husband is covering your children. Refer to Chapter 2 for advice on how to shop for several types of insurance, including life, health, and disability. As with widowed women, COBRA laws dictate that if you are covered by your spouse's company plan, you should be able to continue the same health coverage for at least 18 months, but you will be responsible for paying the premiums. After that, it's up to you to find a comprehensive policy that is affordable.

DECISIONS THAT WILL IMPACT YOUR FINANCIAL WELL-BEING

You'll be called upon to make some decisions that will affect your future financial health.

WHAT TO DO WITH THE HOUSE

Consider selling the house. For some reason, we all want to hang on to the house. Although it represents stability and the memory of happier times, it's also an incredible financial drain for someone living on one income. It provides zero income. There are monthly mortgage payments, upkeep, and thousands of dollars in annual property taxes and insurance that crop up month after month. For divorcées, selling the house and splitting the proceeds with your ex is usually the best way to go. Then you can rent or buy a smaller place.

GO FOR THE PENSION

As a divorced spouse, you are typically entitled to a portion of any retirement benefits earned by your ex during your marriage. In order to get a cut of his retirement plan— either a pension, a 401(k), or an IRA—you'll need a lawyer to petition a state court for a *qualified domestic relations order,* or QDRO (pronounced "quadro"), for a judge to approve. This is an order from the court that explains to a pension plan administrator how to divide the benefits between yourself and your spouse. There are several options, including a one-time payment, monthly payouts at retirement, or a lump-sum payment that you transfer directly into your own IRA where your money will continue to grow tax-free until you retire.

Divorcing women often pass up their soon-to-be ex's pension in favor of the house or up-front cash they can use today. But someone earning around $70,000 a year today could easily retire with a lifetime pension of $1 million or more, depending on the number of years he or she has paid in.

TIMING

As devious as it sounds, it pays to time your divorce well to maximize your financial position. As long as you have been married for at least 10 years and don't remarry, you can qualify for Social Security benefits based on your ex-spouse's earnings when you both reach age 62, even if he has remarried or hasn't yet retired and begun to receive benefits himself.

The rules do say that your Social Security benefits based on your own work history must be less than half of his benefits at age 65. You must also have been divorced for at least two years to make a claim. So try to drag out the marriage for at least 10 years—even if he wants out after 9½ years. And remember, even if you are on decent terms with your ex-spouse when the time comes, you should plan to collect this benefit. Doing so won't reduce his payout at all, and he'll never even know when you start receiving Social Security checks.

TAX TIPS

- You should file your income tax to the IRS as a *single* (not as married filing jointly) if your divorce is finalized by year-end.

- Part of your attorney's fees might be tax deductible, so keep an itemized record of your bills. This is typically possible for any tax advice they gave you.

- Should your spouse agree to provide alimony payments or money to maintain your home and life each month, you'll probably be required to pay taxes on that income. Those payments, however, are tax-deductible for your former spouse.

- He may agree not to call the payments "alimony." In that case, you avoid taxes, but he misses the deduction. To get him to agree, you might be able to compromise on a smaller amount so you'll both benefit.

- Alimony income may be considered as "earned income" to you. If so, it may be eligible for contributions to an Individual Retirement Account.

- Since there are no taxes taken out of those alimony checks, you probably will have to file quarterly tax returns on the funds. Your accountant can estimate that amount for you and provide you with the correct forms.

- If you have children, you may qualify for head-of-household status and be eligible to use the dependent exemption, thereby cutting your tax bite. You have to be named as the custodial parent in the divorce decree to do so.

- Child support is not taxed as income, nor can your ex deduct it.

- You may be eligible for child care tax credits as well. Child care includes day care, nursery school, and even kindergarten. Your credit is determined by the amount you pay for child care and your *adjusted gross income* (income on which your federal taxes are computed). In general, if you have one child under the age of 13 in day care, the first $2,400 you spend qualifies. If you have two or more children under that age in day care, the first $4,800 qualifies. The total credit drops, though, as your income rises. If you earn more than $28,000 a year, for example, you'll get a credit of 20% of your total expenses, capped at the above levels of $2,400 and $4,800. So your highest credit would be $960 for two children. Someone earning under $10,000 is eligible for a 30% credit, or $720 for one child and $1,440 for two or more. The new tax law creates a special credit, beginning in tax year 1998, for parents of a dependent child who is under age 17 at year-end. Only the parent who claims the child as a dependent qualifies. The credit is $400 per child in 1998 and $500 per child after that. The maximum adjusted gross income for an unmarried taxpayer is $75,000. Your child credit will be reduced by $50 for each $1,000 above that limit. All dependent children must have a Social Security number for you to claim them as a dependent.

- Check with your employer to see if there is a dependent care reimbursement plan available. Some employers allow you to set aside as much as $5,000 from your annual pretax income to pay for child care.

- The sum set aside in a reimbursement plan will reduce the amount you can apply for as child care credit. For most people, the reimbursement account is usually the best bet.

- If you decide to keep the house, you won't pay taxes at the time of your divorce settlement, but it may be subject to taxes should you sell it down the road. That can be a serious blow, because you pay taxes on all the appreciation before it was transferred to your sole ownership

(continued)

TAX TIPS (CONTINUED)

and after. Home sellers did get somewhat of a break when President Clinton signed a new tax law in 1997. Currently, individuals are allowed up to $250,000 in tax-free capital gains when they sell their personal home; couples are allowed up to $500,000. Under the old laws, there was a one-time tax break for the value gained up to $125,000, but you had to be 55 to qualify. A *capital gain or loss* is the amount you make or lose when you sell an asset like a home. Documentation is important for tax purposes.

GETTING FINANCIAL ADVICE

Take your time before making major investment decisions with your settlement money. There are all sorts of people out there ready to pounce on your money for their gain, not yours. It's best to let your head clear for a few months before making any major investment decisions. Instead, set the funds aside in certificates of deposit or money market accounts. Even though these accounts pay low interest, they are a safe and relatively liquid place to keep your money while you get up to speed in the world of investing. See Chapter 2 for places to find the best rates on CDs and money market accounts.

Seek financial advice before you agree to terms of a settlement. A good financial planner can help you sort things out without pushing you to make fast decisions about how to invest your settlement money. If you don't already have a financial planner that you trust, you might want to check around with some friends or relatives to see if they have any good recommendations. You can also call the National Association of Personal Financial Advisors (800-366-2732) for a list of fee-only advisors in your town. But don't expect the planner to make your decisions for you. You are solely responsible for your choices now. In Chapter 5, we will discuss in more detail how to choose a planner.

Hire a good accountant. Divorce and taxes can be messy. An accountant is one professional you would be well-advised to have on board before you agree to any final terms of the divorce.

It's understandable if all this seems like more than you can handle, so take it easy and go one step at a time. In the next chapter, we'll show you how to develop a budget that works for you.

CHAPTER FOUR

A Budget That Works

F inding the essential papers and taking those first steps toward financial independence are difficult chores at best. Money issues are such a distant second to your emotional stress right now. Unfortunately, this is the time you've got to press ahead. In the end, you'll be grateful you did. Developing a sensible, personally customized budget will allow you to take control of your spending and make your financial life secure. Don't be surprised, though, if for the first six months or so your monthly spending and budgeting is all over the map. Eventually, things will settle into place and it will be easier to anticipate your monthly spending and saving needs.

You've already assembled the most important documents and set up shop in your makeshift office. Laid out in front of you is the data that will help you get your budget together. Essentially, you must determine how to allocate your incoming funds to satisfy your spending needs while continuing to protect and build your nest egg for your retirement, for your children's education, to support elderly parents, or other future money demands.

The most important thing to remember is that this is not a time to be careless with your funds or to hand over all the decisions to someone else. It's *your* life, *your* money, and *your* responsibility. Moreover, it's definitely not the time to spend on nonessential items to make yourself feel better for a while in a superficial way.

I have known dozens of widows and divorcées who felt compelled to spend on everything from a new car to a new wardrobe to a long vacation. It made them feel better. It gave them a fresh start of sorts. Try to resist this splurge mentality. You need to hang onto your money right now, not blow it frivolously. There will come a time when you can do something nice for yourself, but that time is not now.

And don't be surprised if you're suddenly asked for a loan by a friend or relative. People figure that if you've come into some money you'll be more than happy to tide them over for a spell. Unless it's a desperate situation, say you're sorry, but no. This money is all you have left to make sure you have a solid financial future.

As things settle down, you might discover you're better off than you feared. Nonetheless, the first few months will be touch and go emotionally and financially. You'll probably find that it pays to curtail your spending until your husband's estate is settled, or until your divorce decree is final, and for several months thereafter until you have a good understanding of your flow of funds.

For this exercise, you'll want to start a new notebook and a fresh folder. This is not for your husband's estate stuff or your divorce papers. You're about to develop a budget for your present money situation and your future one. It requires you to focus on how you spend your money, make your money, and save your money. It's your financial snapshot, so be as careful as you can in itemizing your expenses and income so you can devise an honest budget that will work for you. Budgeting doesn't have to be a painful procedure, but it will take some motivation. Think of it as your blueprint for financial security—one that will allow you to meet your most important goals.

CALCULATING YOUR NET WORTH

Widows will first want to determine the total value of all assets now available to them. Divorced women should already have done this in order to come to an equitable divorce settlement. After you've identified your assets and liabilities, then you can figure out how much you spend and how much you have coming in. Your assets are things of value that you actually own such as your home, jewelry, a car. Liabilities are obligations to pay, such as loans or credit card debts. Your income consists of your salary or other earnings from freelance or part-time work, plus funds you receive from investments such as interest on money market accounts, rental income, or dividends from stocks and mutual fund holdings.

Fill in the worksheet in Figure 4.1 to help you find out what you are worth today. This will serve as your *balance sheet,* or record of your current net worth.

By subtracting your total liabilities from your total assets you'll have a rough idea of what you have to work with. Some of your assets are not readily available to you (for example, your home's value), and others represent cash on hand that you can use to pay immediate household expenses. Don't get panicky if your outstanding debts seem overwhelming. Your next step is to create a spending and saving budget that will help you find ways to augment your income and rein in your spending.

FIGURE 4.1 YOUR NET WORTH

ASSETS: WHAT YOU OWN

Your annual income: $_____

Savings account balance: $_____

Checking account balance: $_____

Treasury bonds: $_____

Certificates of deposit: $_____

Money market accounts: $_____

Value of your home: $_____

Value of any other real estate: $_____

Life insurance payout from your husband's employer: $_____

Other life insurance policies: $_____

Your husband's pension payout: $_____

Your pension's value: $_____

IRA: $_____

Keogh: $_____

Cash value of your life insurance: $_____

Value of any stocks you now own: $_____

Value of any bonds you now own: $_____

Value of any mutual funds you own: $_____

Other investments: $_____

FIGURE 4.1 (CONTINUED)

ASSETS: WHAT YOU OWN

Business interests: $_____

Value of car(s): $_____

Your furnishings: $_____

Your clothes: $_____

Your jewelry: $_____

Total assets: _____

LIABILITIES: WHAT YOU OWE

What you owe on your house or rental agreement: $_____

Home equity loans outstanding: $_____

Credit card balances: $_____

Car loan or lease payments remaining: $_____

Education loans outstanding: $_____

Yearly car insurance payment: $_____

Health insurance payment: $_____

Homeowner's or renter's insurance owed: $_____

Annual property taxes: $_____

Federal income tax: $_____

State income tax: $_____

City income tax: $_____

FIGURE 4.1 (CONTINUED)

LIABILITIES: WHAT YOU OWE

Annual electric bill: $_____

Annual gas bill: $_____

Annual phone bill: $_____

Estimated yearly clothing costs: $_____

Estimated transportation expenses: $_____

Annual car upkeep and gasoline expenses: $_____

Annual tuition expenses for self: $_____

Annual tuition expenses for children: $_____

Annual medical bills not covered by insurance: $_____

Children's clothing expenses: $_____

Estimated yearly grocery bills: $_____

Estimated annual travel expenses: $_____

Other liabilities: $_____

Total liabilities: $_____

Net worth = total assets − total liabilities = $_____

HOW MUCH INCOME DO YOU HAVE?

Let's start with the plus side of your plan. Your mission is to follow the money trail. What money do you have coming in each month? Are there one-time cash injections you expect to have to invest? In addition to their own income, widows will probably have future income from their husband's estate in the way of Social Security, life insurance payments, employer pension funds, and the like. Divorcing women might have some form of ongoing spousal support or a monetary division of assets. You might not receive some of these funds for a period of time until things are settled. Make a note of when you can expect to see that cash. Until then, you'll need to rely on your cash reserves or perhaps even borrow funds, which makes watching your spending in these early days extremely important.

Fill in the worksheet in Figure 4.2 and you'll have a pretty good idea of how much you take in.

HOW MUCH DO YOU SPEND
EACH MONTH?

Now you've got to scrutinize your bills. That means poring over your spending history for the past year. You'll need your credit card statements and checking account records to get a good read on this. Don't forget to include cash expenditures. Expenses that were covered with cash are tough to follow, but do your best to ferret them out.

Divide the bills into categories: housing expenditures (monthly mortgage, rent, etc.), entertainment, autos, food, utilities, and so on. Then analyze your findings for ways that you can trim spending. Entertainment expenses, for example, are pretty easy to pare, but utility bills are not so easy to cut.

FIGURE 4.2 INCOME WORKSHEET

SOURCES OF INCOME	AMOUNT $
Your net income (gross minus taxes)	
Insurance income	
Investment income interest, dividends	
Pension income	
Social Security	
Alimony	
Child support	
Proceeds from sale of home or other real estate	
Other freelance income	
TOTAL (income)	

You'll discover that you have two types of monthly expenses: There are *fixed expenses* that you are obligated to pay each month, no matter what (for example, your mortgage or electric bill). Then there are those *variable expenses* that fluctuate month to month (such as your dry cleaning bill or health club dues).

THE CORE BILLS

Core bills are the ones you pay regularly for a set period of time. They might be due annually, monthly, or quarterly, but whatever the interval, they are commitments you made that you are obligated to pay, at least for now. They usually include your mortgage, utility bills, and taxes. Down the road, you'll more than likely be able to cut even these expenses dramatically. Obviously, you won't need two cars anymore if you're a widow—unless you have kids who need wheels, of course. But you may also have new expenses such as your therapist bills. You may move to a smaller home that has more affordable upkeep, a smaller mortgage, slimmer property taxes, and lower water and electric bills. Your phone bill for one person should definitely be lower than it was for two people, your insurance payments will be reduced, and so forth. But for now, record what is currently due to help plan your budget for the next few months.

Complete the worksheet in Figure 4.3 and tote up your fixed expenses.

OPTIONAL SPENDING

There are expenses that change each month, and these are the ones you have the most control over immediately. By sorting through your past year's worth of checks and other forms of payment, you're going to get a pretty good picture of where you splurged and where you didn't. Maybe you'll find you shelled out $150 every two months for a haircut and highlighting. Maybe you spent $100 a month on dry cleaning. Other such optional expenses include health club memberships, vacations, magazine subscriptions, movies, meals out, and groceries, all of which change frequently and are likely to continue to be variable in the months to come. You can start cutting back on these costs today. Getting a handle on your spending will help you set priorities and allow you to start saving aggressively. The bottom line is that you have to be ruthless about cutting back wherever you can.

FIGURE 4.3 YOUR CURRENT EXPENSES— FIXED OUTFLOW

EXPENSE	AMOUNT $	WHEN DUE	HOW OFTEN DUE: MONTHLY, QUARTERLY, ANNUALLY
Car payment			
Gas bill			
Co-op/condo fee			
Electric bill			
Insurance premiums: Auto Homeowner Life Health Disability			
Loan payments			
Telephone bills			
Mortgage			
Water bill			
Federal taxes			
Self-employed taxes			
State taxes			
Property taxes			
TOTAL (fixed expenses)			

Complete the worksheet in Figure 4.4. This will give you an idea of where you can cut back on spending.

YOUR CASH FLOW

To determine your monthly cash flow, subtract your total expenses from your total income. That should give you a rough idea of what you have to work with each month. This is not an exact science, but the exercise should help you get a grip on where you stand today and help you set your future money goals.

The next stage is to track your current spending for the next two months on a daily basis. To do so, you'll want to make sure you save all your receipts and make entries on a daily basis so you don't inadvertently leave something out. You might want to set some goals for yourself as well. You might, for instance, try to squeeze $20 out of your current expenses to put into a personal fund for yourself. Then, if you are able to save that sum each month, in a few months you can reward yourself with something special just for you, maybe a half day at a spa or a trip to the theater to see a show. You could also opt for some more serious goal setting. After her husband died, Susan, then 36, decided her goals were to study nursing and to buy a house in five years. For now, she is still living in the house she rented with her husband.

Here are a few rules to keep in mind when setting your goals and planning for your future financial health:

- Your mortgage or rent payments each month should add up to less than 30% of your monthly net income.

- Your total debt, excluding your mortgage, should be less than 20% of your net income.

FIGURE 4.4 OPTIONAL EXPENSES

EXPENSE	TOTAL FOR THE YEAR	AVERAGE PER MONTH
Car expenses: gas, repair, etc.		
Clothing		
Cosmetics		
Computer hardware and software		
Child care		
Charity		
Bank fees		
Eating out		
Hairdresser		
Drugstore items		
Prescription drugs		
Tuition		
Household help		
Club memberships		
Gifts		
Unreimbursed medical bills		

FIGURE 4.4 (CONTINUED)

EXPENSE	TOTAL FOR THE YEAR	AVERAGE PER MONTH
Vacations		
Public transportation		
Household items: furniture, curtains, etc.		
Groceries		
Alcohol		
Entertaining		
Automatic savings plans: 401(k) contribution		
Movies		
Other entertainment outside the home		
Hobbies		
Legal fees		
Accountant fees		
Credit card finance charges		
Subscriptions to magazines, newspapers		
Books		

FIGURE 4.4 (CONTINUED)

EXPENSE	TOTAL FOR THE YEAR	AVERAGE PER MONTH
Pet care and supplies		
Dry cleaning and laundry		
Misc. expenses		
TOTAL (optional expenses)		

- Most financial planners recommend that you save at least 10% of your income each month for your retirement, although women typically save just 1.5% and men 3%.

For women who are computer literate, there are several good software programs that can help you set up a budget and manage your money. We'll discuss on-line services in more detail in Chapter 9. Some personal finance programs worth checking out are Kiplinger's Simply Money, Managing Your Money, Microsoft Money, Quicken, and Wealthbuilder. The programs cost around $40 to $50. You'll have to spend some time up front inputting all the financial information, but ultimately these programs can make managing your money and budgeting fairly straightforward. They allow you to pay your bills electronically, balance your checkbook, and quickly generate charts showing how you are spending your money. They also provide spreadsheets that let you estimate monthly payments on loans and forecast future budgets by testing various spending scenarios.

In the next chapter, you'll learn how to seek out professional help to put together a financial plan for the next year, or for 5, 10, or more years down the line.

CHAPTER FIVE

$

Getting Financial Advice

As Agatha Christie once wrote, "Those who never think of money need a great deal of it." Maybe you are fortunate enough to have enough money to live on comfortably for the rest of your life. But chances are, even if your husband left you with substantial assets, you'll still need to prepare yourself to manage those funds so they will always be there for you. Your goal is to protect those assets and make them grow for your future and your children's.

No one is going to look after your money the way you can. It's yours to lose. So you have to make it your responsibility to understand the investment process and make decisions about how you want to invest your money.

You might not think so, but you *are* ready to manage your own money. It's time to take charge. This is not rocket science, but it can be complicated. Over time, though, it's a skill you can learn and master. It just takes a disciplined approach and an ability to handle some risk—something many women find hard to do.

Now that you've figured out your net worth and established a budget, it's time to put your assets to work. Your goal is to have a nice mix of stocks and bonds that provide a balanced portfolio suitable for your age and future money needs. Certainly there's a bit of luck involved, but there is nothing mystical or magical about investing successfully. You can develop a financial plan and investment strategy to ensure that you will never lack for money. Chapter 6 will explain the universe of investment opportunities from which you may choose, but for now you will probably want to get some money advisors on your team. In time, you will be confident enough to handle your own affairs quite nicely.

THE FIRST YEAR

Go slowly! The first year is difficult. You have just lost a spouse. Your entire world is collapsing. Your secure financial world is going completely haywire (along with everything else) and you don't know what to deal with first.

After you've negotiated your way through the must-do list and located crucial documents, take a break. Even though you will feel pressured to make major financial decisions quickly, most financial advisors recommend that you resist doing so. These are emotionally trying times, and you are probably not yet prepared to make wise decisions. So procrastinate for six months to a year (preferably a full year) and use the time to get up to speed on personal finances. You may lose some potential short-term gains, but you're not ready to make a move that might cost you the financial assets you have gained from your husband's estate or divorce settlement. This is one time when playing it safe will serve you well.

You'll have the funds invested (no under-the-mattress plan here) but it will be stashed in liquid bank savings accounts, certificates of deposit, money market accounts, or Treasury bills. These investments will guarantee your principal and pay you a modest amount of interest, say, 5% to 6% a year for a one-year CD. See Chapter 2 for a list of institutions with top-yielding CDs and money market accounts.

For the long term, these kinds of investments are far too conservative (we'll get into this in depth later), but until you can make clearheaded choices, you're better off taking the conservative route. Whatever you do, ignore any unsolicited tips or advice from well-intentioned friends and relatives. Nine times out of ten the investments will be completely inappropriate for you.

When you are ready to take action, it is a good idea to set up an appointment with a financial advisor to help you develop a short- and a long-term investment plan. In the first several months of being on your own, your priorities are paying your bills and getting a handle on your financial situation. After six months or so, you should be ready to start taking a closer look at your assets and investments to see if they are going to be able to meet your future financial goals.

You'll want to be sure that you set up a master file to keep track of any paperwork generated by your new active role in your financial plans. All your brokerage account papers should go in one file and should include monthly account records, all buy and sell slips, and any reports from the companies whose shares you own. For tax purposes, you'll also need to keep records of any dividend payments and capital gains generated by the securities. In the end, *planning your financial future is solely your responsibility,* but you don't have to do it alone.

SELECTING A FINANCIAL ADVISOR

Putting together a financial plan takes time and plenty of patience. That's why for many women in your situation, it's a smart idea to seek out a professional to help you get your plan in motion. There are a myriad of people out there who bill themselves as financial advisors. These include financial advisors, financial consultants, financial planners, life insurance agents, money managers, and stockbrokers, among many others. They all have something to sell to you.

And the array of investment choices is staggering: dozens of bonds, from zero-coupon bonds to government bonds to junk bonds to bunny bonds; thousands of different mutual funds that invest everything from real estate to foreign currencies; and, of course, a mind-boggling number of companies that sell shares of their stock on the public exchanges. The sheer scope of investment choices today makes a convincing argument for hiring a reliable advisor who can help you make sense of it all, at least early on. But who should you pick for that critical mission, and where will you find the best candidate for the job? Your first move is to make sure you understand the different types of advisors, what they can do for you, and what you will pay for that service.

WHAT YOU NEED TO KNOW ABOUT FINANCIAL PLANNERS

A financial planner will typically charge you something, perhaps $500 to $1,000, for a basic financial plan. But that might be well worth it should you find someone who offers unbiased advice about the best course of action for your unique situation. It doesn't have to be any more than just a road map, so to speak. It will allow you to create a future financial scenario for yourself. Right now, you just have your current snapshot of what's in place today.

Your planner's job is to take stock of your entire financial universe from the materials you provide, such as your statement of net worth and your monthly budget. Then, based on your stated objectives and goals—you need to pay for a child's college education, you want to go back to graduate school, you want to buy a vacation home, you want to retire in 15 years, and so forth—the planner will help you fashion an overall financial strategy not restricted to investments only.

The plan should cover the gamut, from taxes to investments to estate planning issues, and should be fairly comprehensive. Moreover, you should expect it to contain recommendations for specific investments, with their future returns projected. Your planner should also be able to give you advice on your insurance needs and get your estate plan in motion. We'll discuss more about estate planning and the importance of wills in Chapter 8. If all goes well, you will have an ongoing relationship with the planner and receive quarterly statements reviewing your financial situation. Then, too, you'll probably meet once or twice a year to make changes and adjustments.

Finding a good financial planner whom you can trust with your finances can be tricky, though. For the most part, the industry is unregulated, which means that it's hard to figure out who is a legitimate advisor. In general, you're better off if you work with a *fee-only planner.* There are more than 4,000 of these individuals currently practicing.

Fee-only planners charge you an up-front fee for their advice. It can be a percentage of your portfolio (say 1% to 3%), a per-hour charge, or a basic fee per planning session. They don't, however, make any commissions from the investments they recommend. To get a list of fee-only planners in your area, call the National Association of Personal Financial Advisors (800-366-2732). You'll also want to ask for referrals from friends or other professionals you work with, such as your attorney or accountant.

The key is to feel comfortable with the planner and assured that he or she has your best interests in mind. The more sophisticated you are about investing, the less hand-holding you will need. It pays to spend some time meeting and interviewing at least three potential planners. Doing so will give you a better feel for the kind of advice you're likely to get, and you'll sense what kind of person you'll click with.

Another type of planner is a *fee-plus-commission planner.* These planners typically bill you a set fee *and* earn commissions on some of the investments they recommend to you. Then there are *commission-only planners.* They are similar to stockbrokers and insurance agents in that they earn a commission on the investments you buy through them. Their employer pays them to push the product to you. This is not necessarily bad, but it does pose the question of whether there is a conflict of interest. Are they just telling you to buy something so they can land a sweet commission, or is it really a good product for you? If the investment turns out to be a solid performer, it hardly matters if they get paid for their advice that way. But if it goes sour, it could leave you with a bad taste in your mouth.

It's important to seek out advisors or planners who have a *Certified Financial Planner* (CFP) accreditation. A CFP is a professional who has completed a rigorous series of courses and exams in financial planning and undergoes 15 hours of continuing education each year. The CFP is awarded by the International Board of Standards and Practices for the Denver-based Institute of Certified Financial Planners. To access a database of 7,000-plus planners with the CFP credential, call 800-282-7526. They can send you a list of CFPs in your town. Another organization that can provide you with names of planners is the International Association for Financial Planning (IAFP), which offers a free guide called *Consumer Guide to Comprehensive Financial Planning* and will mail you a list of five planners in your area who have been in business for at least three years and have referrals from six clients (call 800-945-4237).

You'd be well advised to place a call to the *Securities and Exchange Commission*'s information line (202-942-8088) and the *National Association of Securities Dealers* (800-289-9999) to be certain that whomever you are working with is registered as "someone who gives advice about securities for compensation." Meantime, make sure there are no complaints filed against the professional you choose.

HIRING A FULL-SERVICE STOCKBROKER

A *brokerage* is, quite simply, an intermediary between buyers and sellers of stocks and other securities. Until recently, women got little respect from stockbrokers. Brokers frequently snubbed women in favor of men, whom they perceived to have more money to invest than women and, therefore, were more worthy of their time. A few years ago, *Money* magazine conducted a survey of 21 brokerages and found that when men and women with the same amount to invest walked off the street into a broker's office, the men got far more attention than did the women. The men received an average of 47 minutes of time with a broker, while women were given just 38 minutes. Moreover, the survey found that 25% of the time, brokers did not even ask women about their investment histories, as compared to 10% of the male customers.

But that's all changing. Since 1991, more than a dozen big firms—including Merrill Lynch, Oppenheimer Funds, Prudential Securities, Salomon Smith Barney, and The Resnick Group in Beverly Hills—have set up departments that offer investment advice specifically for women. "Over the years, I have found that women aren't prepared to make important financial decisions, or fail to understand the financial consequences of decisions they've made, or of those made for them," says Judy Resnick, CEO of The Resnick Group. "The Resnick Group was founded to provide women with the investment education, knowledge, and guidance needed to make informed decisions about their money."

The programs provide free financial literature and are staffed by brokers who specialize in women's issues. Salomon Smith Barney now boasts that a third of its account holders are women. And at Oppenheimer, the number of women account holders has more than tripled since the early 1990s. So you might want to consider one of these female-friendly firms for a broker you'll want to work with.

Before you select a stockbroker to execute your financial transactions, you should understand just how he or she expects to be paid for this service and how you can cut those costs. A broker earns his or her income by the commissions paid on investments you buy or sell. Typically, you will pay a commission of 2% or so on any securities that you buy and sell. If you buy, say 100 shares of a $30 stock, you might pay around $80 in commissions. Moreover, full-service brokers usually make the highest commissions on the riskier investments like options or limited partnerships.

It's sometimes uncomfortable to talk about money and, especially, compensation issues. But don't be timid about asking your broker how he or she is to be paid for a particular investment. Anything higher than a 5% commission should set off alarm bells in your head.

This is not the time for you to be playing around with high-risk investments. While you are beginning to move your funds out of conservative certificates of deposit, you should stick to a somewhat cautious strategy for a while longer and slowly add riskier choices to your mix. Meantime, watch out for brokers who recommend frequent transactions, called *churning* your account. For most of us, buying and holding for at least a three-year time horizon is usually more appropriate. But brokers make money on every trade they make, so they have an incentive to keep it rolling.

Meanwhile, you could be eligible for some discounts on commissions. Some brokers lower commissions by around 1% on in-house mutual funds if you invest a minimum of $25,000 or so in one fund. Also, buying in lots of 100 shares at a time should lower the fee. Then, too, brokerages will frequently offer discounts of 40% or more to their best customers—in other words, someone with a hefty sum under their management. If you really want to shave commissions, you can trade through a discount brokerage house like Charles Schwab or Quick & Reilly and lower fees by 70% or so. Moneywise, women can cut even those low commissions by another 60% to 80% by executing their own trades directly over the Internet with one of the growing number of on-line brokerages like E*Trade, ebroker, or eSchwab. Commissions range from under $10 to $40 to trade up to 1,000 shares. We'll discuss on-line investing in detail in Chapter 9.

But don't expect to receive any investment advice or additional services from discount brokerages. When you hire a full-service broker, you receive extra attention. For example, you can request research reports from the brokerage's analysts, as well as other detailed research reports from firms like Morningstar and Value Line. Moreover, your broker should be available to meet with you one-on-one at least every four months to go over your investments.

As with planners, it's smart to ask for recommendations from colleagues and other people you respect. You might also check with women you've met through support groups and the like who have found a broker who understands their special needs. Again, you'll want to interview two or three brokers to see what kinds of investments they would suggest given your situation. You should also do your due diligence by calling the National Association of Securities Dealers to make sure the broker is licensed to operate in your state and has not had any complaints or disciplinary action filed against him or her. Never be swayed by a broker who cold-calls you at home offering investment tips. Be sure you understand how to read your account statements so you can keep careful records of any transactions. Then, too, do your own independent research before handing over any funds. (See Figure 5.1.)

If for any reason you have a dispute with your broker, fight back fast. You will need to discuss it with the broker directly, talk to his or her manager, and write a letter to the firm's regulatory compliance officer. You must, however, be able to prove beyond a doubt that the broker invested your money without your permission or in securities that were unsuitable for you. You typically have two years to file a claim. The National Association of Securities Dealers can give you more information on how to get your problem corrected. Increasingly, arbitration has become a successful route for small investors seeking to right a wrong.

Most cases are handled by the New York Stock Exchange and the NASD. Fees for filing start at $15. The American Arbitration Association, which has no connection to the industry, holds hearings in most major cities. The filing fees are much higher, though, starting around $300. For more information on filing a claim, contact the NASD (125 Broad Street, New York, NY 10004, 212-480-4881); The NYSE (11 Wall Street, New York, NY 10005, 212-656-2804; or the American Stock Exchange (86 Trinity Place, New York, NY 10006, 212-306-1000).

GOING FOR A MONEY MANAGER

To hire your own personal money manager, you will probably need to have upward of $60,000 to invest. Your broker or financial planner may be able to recommend someone reputable to you. Some banks and brokerages offer what's called

FIGURE 5.1 CONFIRMATION STATEMENT

The confirmation statement you get from your broker after you buy or sell a security spells out the details of a trade. The type of transaction, the exchange where the trade was made and the terms and conditions are explained on the back. You should keep all transaction confirmations as part of your tax records.

Most brokerages are covered by the Securities Investor Protection Corporation (SIPC), which insures your account up to $500,000.

The Securities and Exchange Commission (SEC) imposes a fee on most transactions. Some brokerages impose a modest handling charge as well.

You pay brokers' commissions every time you buy or sell stock. The charges are added to the amount you pay when you buy, and deducted when you sell.

The net amount includes the cost of the security plus commissions and fees.

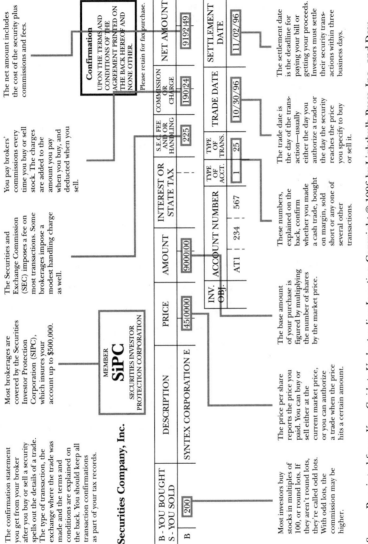

Most investors buy stocks in multiples of 100, or round lots. If they aren't round lots, they're called odd lots. With odd lots, the commission may be higher.

The price per share reports the price you paid. You can buy or sell either at the current market price, or you can authorize a trade when the price hits a certain amount.

The base amount of your purchase is figured by multiplying the number of shares by the market price.

These numbers, explained on the back, confirm whether you made a cash trade, bought on margin, sold short or any one of several other transactions.

The trade date is the day of the transaction—usually either the day you authorize a trade or the day the security reaches the price you specify to buy or sell it.

The settlement date is the deadline for paying your bill or getting your proceeds. Investors must settle their security transactions within three business days.

Source: Reprinted from *Your Guide to Understanding Investing.* Copyright © 1996 by Lightbulb Press, Inc., and Dow Jones & Co., Inc. Used with permission.

a *wrap account*. Here's how it works: The manager will charge an annual fee of around 3% of the sum invested. As you might expect, the more money you give them to manage, the lower the percentage in fees. You'll be billed on a quarterly basis in most cases. You won't pay commissions, however, on any investments you buy or sell. And in most cases, you agree to let the manager make transactions without your approval. In general, having a money manager monitor your portfolio is not the best route to go, because, by the very nature of the relationship, you are handing over the responsibility for your funds to someone else. As we've discussed before, taking an active role is the best way to ensure your financial future is healthy.

Choosing the right money advisor takes legwork, and you have to follow your own instincts about the individual. It's a gut feeling. There are thousands of shady operators out there who are more than happy to review your finances and take your money. They gleefully line their own pockets, not yours. Then, too, a broker or planner who works beautifully with your friend or your Aunt Ann might not have the expertise to handle your situation, or you could have a personality conflict that makes it hard to communicate.

Communication is paramount, though. Revealing your most intimate money profile to a stranger takes trust and confidence. It makes you feel vulnerable in some way. Take whatever time you need to find the right individual. This is a business decision. It's not personal. Your advisor doesn't have to be your confidant, but he or she does have to be someone you can talk to face-to-face and not someone who talks down to you or is condescending in any fashion. After all, you're the customer. You deserve that respect.

Having a competent broker, money manager or planner can make the transition to financial independence smoother than if you were to attempt to navigate the way completely on

QUESTIONS TO ASK A POTENTIAL INVESTMENT ADVISOR

- How long have you been a planner?
- How many years have you worked for this firm?
- Can you tell me some details about the firm's history and the areas you specialize in?
- What are your qualifications?
- What professional groups do you belong to?
- Do you take part in any continuing education programs? How often?
- What percentage of your clients are women?
- What percentage are divorced?
- What percentage are widowed?
- How big are your client's portfolios on average?
- How are you paid?
- What is your area of strength from an investment perspective?
- What is your money philosophy?
- Are you registered with the Securities and Exchange Commission?
- Can you give me three references?
- What was your worst investment last year?
- What was your best investment in the past 12 months?
- How do your contracts work? Are they written or oral?
- Are there any restrictions on terminating your services?
- What can I expect from you in the way of services?
- How often will we meet?
- Based on what you know about my financial situation and objectives, what types of investments do you think would be appropriate, and over what time horizon?

QUESTIONS THE PROFESSIONAL ADVISOR SHOULD ASK YOU

- How old are you?
- How long have you been divorced? Widowed?
- Do you have any dependents?
- What are your assets?
- What are your liabilities?
- What is your total income?
- What are you likely to receive in alimony?
- How much did you receive in insurance payouts from your spouse's estate?
- What is the current value of your home?
- Do you rent?
- What are your housing costs each month?
- What are your total expenses each month?
- What are your goals and objectives?
- Do you have a will in place?
- Do you have life insurance?
- What other insurance coverage do you have—health, automobile, homeowner's?
- What is your money philosophy?
- Are you a conservative investor or are you willing to tolerate some risk?
- Are you savvy about investing?
- How much money management can you handle by yourself?
- What will you need a professional to help you with?
- What benefits does your employer provide?

- How much have you saved in retirement accounts?
- Will you inherit money one day?
- Do you expect to remarry in the next year or so?
- Are you planning to go back to school?

your own. It can also save loads of time that might be better spent on other duties. Nonetheless, the key to a successful partnership is going to be your own involvement and understanding of the decisions you are making that will affect you and your family for years to come. Chapter 6 will give you a crash course in investing, and you'll begin to get clearer understanding about the specific kinds of investments you are going to be selecting.

CHAPTER SIX

$

Investing 101

If you've followed the advice in this book and put your lump-sum insurance payout or divorce settlement funds in low-paying certificates of deposit, money market accounts, or Treasury bills, good for you. You've avoided making any hasty decisions. If you have no investing experience, you'll want to use the next several months to learn about investing, even if you are working with a financial pro.

It's not as hard as you might think. But it's worthy of as much of your attention as you can spare. Before you start actively handling your money, you need to be sure that you are financially literate.

One good way to start educating yourself is to get into the habit of reading the financial pages of your local newspaper and poring over the *Wall Street Journal,* either at the library or by subscribing for a few months or more. You might even consider subscribing to a personal finance magazine such as *Kiplinger's Personal Finance* or *Money,* which are aimed at teaching people about investing in a plain, straightforward manner that they can grasp without too much effort. Your goal is to familiarize yourself with the various terms. Yes, it's jargon, but it's jargon worth learning. Again, even if you use the services of a financial planner or money manager to help put together an investment plan, that doesn't mean you can afford to remain clueless about your finances.

You may not want to take on the financial responsibility of learning to invest. Ignore it long enough and it will go away, right? Just hand it all over to Cousin So-and-so, who purports to have all the answers and a bag of can't-miss investments for you. *Don't.* Taking charge of your finances while you are grieving the loss of a spouse is not something anyone is eager to do, but you may pay dearly for not doing so.

The kinds of investments that will work best for you will depend on a variety of factors, but the most important will be your age, the amount of money you have to invest, your debt load, your monthly expenditures, and whether there are others who rely on you to live—perhaps children or elderly parents. There are thousands of ways to invest your money, some far riskier than others, and it's important to know just how much *risk* (which is a measure of possible loss in value) you can take with your money.

For example, investing in stocks can be dicey over the short term. Yet over every 20-year period since 1931, stocks have outperformed interest-paying investments. In fact, no one can afford *not* to invest in stocks these days. (See Figures 6.1 and 6.2.) But unless you're the next Warren Buffett, you might opt for mutual funds to accomplish this goal. Buying and selling individual shares takes nerves of steel and quite a bit of research to know which ones to buy and precisely when to sell.

For the most part, women hate taking on that kind of risk. It's a psychological thing. If an investment flounders, we internalize the loss and blame ourselves, while men are more apt to shrug their shoulders and chalk it up to bad luck or their brokers' mistakes. But making your money work for you

FIGURE 6.1　BUILDING YOUR NEST EGG

RATE OF RETURN	5	10	YEARS 20	30	40
3%	$19,442.50	$42,027.23	$98,736.83	$175,258.12	$278,512.39
5	20,486.83	46,778.79	123,823.89	250,717.91	459,713.57
8	22,190.01	55,249.70	177,884.17	450,088.55	1,054,284.37
10	23,424.71	61,965.61	229,709.07	683,797.60	1,913,034.07

Use this table to see how much you would save over a period of years at various rates of return if you invested $300 a month.

Source: National Association of Investment Clubs. Reprinted with permission.

is critical. Once you understand what investing is all about, you'll have the confidence to do so.

Here are your three key investment objectives: *growth, income,* and *safety.* In general, safety isn't always the best route to take, but there are times in your life when it is the wisest way to go. For instance, you should opt for safety during those first few months after you've started managing your money solo. As time goes on, you can gradually move into more aggressive, higher-growth investments. It's important to have the right mix of stocks, bonds, and cash and to maintain a balanced portfolio that lets your money grow without risking principal.

Before you make any investment, you'll want to make sure you have an understanding of how liquid that investment is. *Liquidity* is a measure of how quickly you can retrieve your funds. You'll also want to know how safe the investment is. What is the likelihood that you won't get your money back at all? And finally, you'll want to know what the investment's *rate of return* is likely to be, or what it will earn. In general, safe

FIGURE 6.2 REGULAR INVESTING CAN LOWER YOUR AVERAGE COST PER SHARE

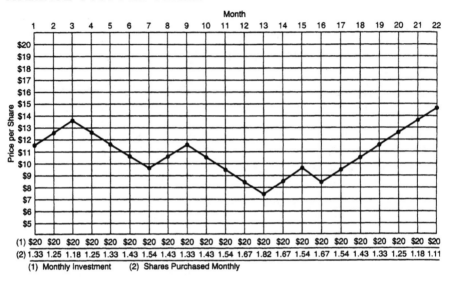

(1) Monthly Investment   (2) Shares Purchased Monthly

If you invested $20 each month in a particular stock, the fluctuating nature of the stock market would allow your $20 investment to buy more of the stock at some times and less of the stock at others. However, because of the nature of dollar cost averaging, you are at an advantage. Your average cost per share is actually lower over time. The figures on the bottom line show the number of shares purchased each month with the $20 fixed amount of investment. The $440 invested over a twenty-two-month period bought 31.228 shares. At the latest price of $18, the 31.228 shares are worth $562.10. As you continue to invest, your advantage will increase.

Source: National Association of Investment Clubs. Reprinted with permission.

investments have the lowest returns and may not even beat inflation in some years.

In general, the percentage of your portfolio invested in stocks or stock mutual funds should be 120 minus your age. The remainder should be divided between bonds and bond mutual funds. When you are in your 30s, you'll aim for long- or intermediate-term bonds. As you grow older, you will shift to fixed-income bonds and then into CDs and money market accounts or funds.

MONEY MARKET ACCOUNTS

These accounts are offered by financial institutions around the country and may require a minimum deposit of up to $2,500. They typically pay a slightly higher, variable interest rate than a plain-vanilla savings account (perhaps 2.5% for a $2,000 investment or 5% for $50,000 or more at the institutions now offering the nation's top rates), and importantly, they are liquid. The account is federally insured and there is no set investment term. Nonetheless, when you take into consideration taxes and inflation, these accounts are usually a poor choice for any significant amount of your portfolio over any lengthy period of time.

FIXED-INCOME INVESTMENTS

Simply put, a fixed-income investment is one that pays you a certain rate of return over a specific time frame. That rate of income doesn't fluctuate when there's bad economic news or other world events that might send the stock market on a tear either up or down. Here are the most common fixed-income investments.

CERTIFICATES OF DEPOSIT (CDs)

A certificate of deposit is a product usually sold by a bank or brokerage house that pays a fixed rate over a fixed term. The time period usually runs from three months to five years. And you are generally required to invest a minimum amount, anywhere from $500 to $2,500. If you have invested through a federally insured institution, the federal government guarantees up to $100,000 through the Federal Deposit Insurance Corporation (FDIC), thus making CDs a very secure investment. If you withdraw your money before the term is over, however, you'll be hit with an early-withdrawal penalty that in the early stages can gobble up part of your principal. The rates CDs pay are typically low—from around 4% or 5% for three-month CDs up to 6% or 7% for two-year CDs.

It's important to do your homework before locking yourself into a CD term. Chances are your local bank is not going to offer you the best rate of return. Personal finance magazines like *Money* and *Kiplinger's Personal Finance* run monthly charts listing the best rates in the country. *USA Today* also runs a regular list of the best rates. And, should you find an attractive rate being offered by a brokerage, you won't be charged a commission. The brokerage gets its payback by charging the bank a fee.

BONDS

This is the biggie. When it comes to fixed-income investments, most people think of bonds, and there are many varieties of them. To put it in the simplest terms, when you buy a bond, you are making a loan to the issuer—the federal government or a corporation. The issuer agrees to pay you a set rate of income, known as the *coupon rate.* That interest is typically paid to you on a quarterly schedule. At the end of the term, the bond matures and you are repaid in full for the principal amount you originally loaned. The key is to hold onto the bonds until *maturity* (the date at which the bond is payable). *Bond rating* services such as A.M. Best (908-439-2200), Standard & Poor's (212-208-1527), and Weiss Group (800-289-9222) rate bonds for safety. The scores for the safest bonds are in the AAA category. The riskiest are listed as Ds. (See Figure 6.3 on pages 86 and 87.)

There are three main types of bonds you can buy. These are government bonds, municipal bonds, and corporate bonds.

GOVERNMENT BONDS

U.S. savings bonds are thought to be the safest bond invest-ments because they are backed by the U.S. government. More-over, the interest, usually 6% or 7% is tax-free. For widows, these bonds are usually a good investment because they offer a steady income stream. There are three different kinds of gov-ernment bonds. *Treasury bills* mature in terms of 60 days to one year. *Treasury notes* have terms of 1 to 10 years. *Treasury bonds* mature in anywhere from 10 to 30 years. Of course, the shorter the term, the lower your interest rate will be. If you are invest-ing in a note with a maturity of less than four years, the mini-mum is $5,000. Otherwise, the minimums are $1,000.

Although investing $20,000 in a three-year Treasury note will get you 7% interest each year and your money back at the end of the term, keep in mind that the $20,000 principal will surely buy less after three years. In essence, you are trad-ing future growth potential for current income.

You can buy these government bonds through a broker, but the U.S. Treasury Department does have a program called Treasury Direct that sells the bonds without a service fee. And you can now have the Treasury deduct the amount you wish to invest directly from your bank account (previously, standard procedure required you to send a certified check or cashier's check). Moreover, you can reinvest the funds from your maturing bonds 24 hours a day, 365 days a year by phone instead of mail. To find out more about the program, contact a Federal Reserve bank near you. To do so, write to the Bureau of Public Debt, Department F, Department of the Treasury, Washington, DC 20239-11200, or call 202-874-4000.

MUNICIPAL BONDS

Municipal bonds are issued by city, local, or state govern-ments. Again, any interest paid by the bonds is free from federal taxes and, if issued by the state in which you live, is

FIGURE 6.3 RATING A BOND: A KEY TO THE CODE

The rating systems of the two major services are similar, but not identical, in the ways they label bond quality. Both services also make distinctions within categories Aa/AA and lower. Moody's uses a numerical system (1,2,3) and Standard & Poor's uses a + or −.

MOODY'S	STANDARD POOR'S	MEANING
Aaa	AAA	Best quality, with the smallest risk; issuers exceptionally stable and dependable
Aa	AA	High quality, with slightly higher degree of long-term risk
A	A	High to medium quality, with many strong attributes but somewhat vulnerable to changing economic conditions
Baa	BBB	Medium quality, currently adequate but perhaps unreliable over long term

INVESTMENT GRADE BONDS

Investment grade generally refers to any bonds rated Baa or higher by Moody's, or BBB by Standard & Poor's.

Ba	BB	Some speculative element, with moderate security but not well safeguarded
B	B	Able to pay now but at risk of default in the future
Caa	CCC	Poor quality, clear danger of default
Ca	CC	Highly speculative quality, often in default
C	C	Lowest-rated, poor prospects of repayment though may still be paying
•	D	In default

JUNK BONDS

Junk bonds are the lowest-rated corporate bonds. There's a greater-than-average chance that the issuer will fail to repay its debt. The highly publicized mergers and takeovers of the 1980s were financed with junk bond issues. Corporations sold high risk bonds to the public. Investors were willing to take the risk because the yields were so much higher than on other, safer bonds.

Source: Reprinted from *The Wall Street Journal Guide to Understanding Money and Investing.* Copyright © 1993 Lightbulb Press, Inc. Used with permission.

additionally spared from state and local taxes. There are two types of municipal bonds: general obligation and general revenue. If the bond is backed by the issuing city or state, it is called *general obligation*. If it is backed by a specific project (for example, a toll road), then it is considered to be *general revenue*.

You should always look for muni bonds that are rated at least A or higher by the rating agencies. You can invest in munis that are guaranteed to repay your principal and any interest earned. These insured bonds are backed by the Municipal Bond Insurance Corporation, or MBIC, and typically don't pay as much interest.

CORPORATE BONDS

Corporate bonds are issued by a corporation. Again, look for the highest ratings possible to shield your investment. Remember, though, the lower-rated bonds will generally pay a higher interest rate. The more risk you take, the more you stand to earn. Your earnings on corporate bonds, paid twice a year, are fully taxable. For the most part, these bonds are purchased in units of $1,000.

Corporate bonds with the lowest ratings are called *junk bonds*. They often have no rating assigned to them at all. The risk here is that the corporation may go belly-up and you are out your entire investment. Chances are you'll want to steer clear of junk bonds completely.

OTHER FIXED-INCOME OPTIONS

Zero-coupon bonds are purchased in face values beginning at $1,000, but they are sold at discounts of as much as 80% of that face value. You receive interest payments only at maturity, but you will be taxed on the annual interest. Since these aren't producing a regular income stream for you, they might not be the best investment choice for you right now.

International bonds, as the name indicates, are issued by foreign corporations and governments. The risk factor with these bonds is that their value will depend on the dollar's relationship to the foreign currency.

Ginnie Maes are another type of fixed-income investment similar to bonds, but they are actually securities that invest in mortgages insured by the federal government and are issued by the Government National Mortgage Association (GNMA). Ginnie Maes are usually a higher-paying instrument than a U.S. Treasury bond. The way they pay out, though, is via monthly payments that combine interest earned (which is taxable) with a percentage of your principal. At maturity, then, you will have already been paid back in full. The minimum amount you can invest is $25,000.

Guaranteed investment contracts (GICs), which have been popular in retirement plans for years, are fixed investments, usually lasting seven years, that yield around 5% and are issued by insurance companies. Some 75% of all 401(k) plans offer GICs as an option. These are not federally insured at all, but are backed by the insurer itself. In reality, the interest is guaranteed only for the initial year. The real drawback to GICs is that they pay so little interest and, over the long haul, are simply *too* safe for most investors.

Another investment option you might want to consider is an *annuity.* Annuities are insurance-backed investments that come in two different flavors. The first is known as an *immediate annuity* because you invest a lump sum and start receiving payments right off the bat. The government will tax the funds as you receive them. But if you aren't in dire need of that cash at the moment, you can choose to defer those payouts to a future date. The amount annuities pay back to you varies widely from insurer to insurer, so you will want to take your time researching the various offerings before investing your funds. With a *deferred annuity,* you can select a fixed interest rate that is guaranteed for a specific time period, and you are taxed only when you start getting income. You can opt for one that is *variable,* where the yield fluctuates according to the performance of the mutual funds in which it is invested. Variable annuities have more upside potential, but again, they do carry more risk.

When it comes to actually withdrawing your money, if you are younger than 59½ and have a deferred annuity, you'll be required to pay a 10% federal tax penalty on any interest earned, and the insurer might slap you with surrender fees of 5% to 15% of your original investment. Regardless of the type of annuity you have, there are several ways you can take money from your annuity. In the *systematic withdrawal* option, you instruct the insurer when to send you checks and the amount you want to receive. In a *life annuity,* the insurer sends you a fixed amount, usually monthly or yearly, for the rest of your life. Once you die, your heirs aren't eligible for any of the funds left in the annuity. You can, however, find annuities that will allow your dependents to get some payouts after you die, but of course, should you opt for this feature, your monthly payout will be lower.

WHAT YOU NEED TO KNOW ABOUT STOCKS

It's true that stocks are far riskier than any of the investments we've discussed so far in this chapter. In general, common stocks have returned 10 to 12% a year since 1926. But you can't ignore the upside potential. In recent years, stocks have returned 20 to 30% annually. Risky or not, you've got to learn to live with them. Put plainly, over the long run, stocks will always outperform fixed-income investments like bonds. But over short time frames they can zig and zag like a roller-coaster ride. When you invest in stocks, you should always do so for a time frame of at least three to five years. Moreover, if you continue to hold a stock investment over time, you reap the benefits of compounding, a combination of your principal investment and subsequent dividends and interest, that keep it growing. Stocks offer you the possibility for growth that everyone needs in order to be financially secure in the future. (See Figure 6.4)

What exactly are stocks? They are shares in a corporation that are sold to generate money for the firm. *Common stock* generally has greater potential for appreciating in value than does preferred stock. Currently, there are some 8,000 companies trading shares on the big three exchanges—the New York Stock Exchange, the American Stock Exchange, and the National Association of Securities Dealers Automatic Quotation system (NASDAQ). One method of tracking the overall health of the stock market is the *Dow Jones Averages*. The Dow Industrial, Composite, Transportation, and Utility averages are indicators of how the stock market is faring. The Industrial for instance, consists of 30 major stocks such as Disney and IBM. There are 20 stocks in the Transportation average, 15 stocks in the Utility average, and 65 in the Composite.

Hundreds of millions of shares are traded daily, and picking the cream of the crop can be difficult at best. When you buy shares from a major brokerage you will usually be charged a commission of 2% or so. Discount brokerages will lower that commission by about 70%, but you shouldn't expect much in the way of service or investment advice for that.

For the more confident do-it-yourself investors, there are more than 300 public companies that allow you to buy shares directly from them without going through a broker at all. You will pay some fees, but in general they are far less imposing. You may also have to make a minimum investment of between $60 and $1,000. Some of the companies offering these direct stock purchase plans include Wal-Mart, Ford Motor Company, and Sony. To get a list of companies that let you buy directly

FIGURE 6.4 THE POWER OF COMPOUNDING

YEAR	STARTING EARLY		STARTING LATER	
	CONTRIBUTION	YEAR-END VALUE	CONTRIBUTION	YEAR-END VALUE
1	$2,000	$2,200		
2	2,000	4,620	$40,000 invested over 20 years	
3	2,000	7,282		
4	2,000	10,212		
5	2,000	13,431		
6	2,000	16,974		
7	2,000	20,871		
8	2,000	25,158	↓	
9	↑	27,674	$2,000	$2,200
10		30,441	2,000	4,620
11	$16,000 invested over 8 years	33,485	2,000	7,282
12		36,834	2,000	10,210
13		40,517	2,000	13,431
14		44,569	2,000	16,974
15		49,026	2,000	20,871
16		53,929	2,000	25,158
17		59,322	2,000	29,874
18		65,254	2,000	35,061
19		71,779	2,000	40,767
20		78,957	2,000	47,044
21		86,853	2,000	53,948
22		95,583	2,000	61,643
23		105,092	2,000	69,897
24		115,601	2,000	79,087
25		127,161	2,000	89,196
26		139,877	2,000	100,316
27		153,865	2,000	112,548
28		169,252	2,000	126,003
Earnings after 35 years		$169,252	Earnings after 25 Years	$126,003

Growth based on a hypothetical 10% rate of return, and does not represent the return of any particular investment.

Source: Reprinted from *Your Guide to Understanding Investing.* Copyright © 1996 by Lightbulb Press, Inc. and Dow Jones & Co., Inc. Used with permission.

from them, write to the National Association of Investors Corporation, 1515 East Eleven Mile Road, Royal Oak, MI 48067. You can also subscribe to the newsletter *No-Load Stock Insider,* $33 for six bimonthly issues, 800-233-5922. You might even consider joining or starting an *investment club,* a group of people who research stocks and pool their money together to invest as one-entity. The NAIC can help you get started. There are 50,000 clubs in the U.S. alone today.

There are four basic types of stocks:

Blue chips are probably the most familiar. These are typically stocks of well-established corporations like AT&T and General Motors. They are considered to be the best-quality investments and will normally pay *dividends,* a payout to shareholders based on profits.

Income stocks will pay even higher dividends to investors, usually anywhere from 50% to 75% of profits four times a year. The stock prices for these companies, often utilities, have stayed fairly flat in the past. Now, however, with deregulation sweeping the nation, mergers between power companies are beginning to change that somewhat.

Small-company stocks are usually the fast growers, but they do carry more risk.

Foreign stocks are a great way to diversify your portfolio. But the risk is compounded by the exchange rate. Hundreds of foreign firms trade here in the form of *American Depository Receipts,* or ADRs. A brokerage house, like Merrill Lynch, can provide more information about specific ADRs.

MUTUAL FUNDS

Stocks are an essential part of a healthy portfolio, so bone up and invest boldly. That said, I personally am nervous when it comes to buying individual stocks. For me, and I suspect for most of you, mutual funds are the way to go. There are now more than 7,000 mutual funds to choose from, and believe me, it's confusing. A *mutual fund* is a selection of bonds and/or stocks that are invested as a pool. They aren't federally insured, but the great thing about mutual funds is that they allow you to diversify your investments, and they are managed by professionals. The total pool of securities is divided into shares and sold to investors like us. (See Figures 6.5 to 6.7.)

In mid-1997, 54% of all mutual fund assets were invested in stock funds, 23% in bond and income funds and 23% in money market funds. Overall, in July of 1997, close to 4.3 billion was invested in 6,746 mutual funds. In most cases, the minimum investment is around $1,500, but you can get into some for less. Once you're in, you can routinely reinvest small amounts on a regular basis. As with stocks, mutual fund share prices, otherwise known as *net asset value,* rise and fall on a daily basis. But since you are investing in a variety of securities, as opposed to having all your money caught up in

FIGURE 6.5 ASSETS IN MUTUAL FUNDS

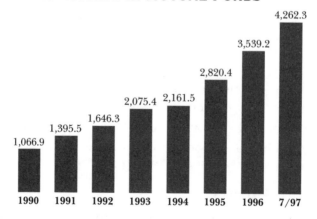

Source: A Guide to Mutual Funds, Investment Company Institute, Washington, D.C. Reprinted with permission.

FIGURE 6.6 HOW MUTUAL FUND ASSETS
ARE INVESTED

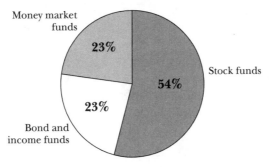

Source: A Guide to Mutual Funds, Investment Company Institute, Washington, D.C.
Reprinted with permission.

one individual company, you have a bit more protection
from market swings.

As with stocks, there is a wide range of fund groups, each
with a different investment objective—safety, growth, or
income. (See Figures 6.8 to 6.11)

FIGURE 6.7 NUMBER OF MUTUAL FUNDS

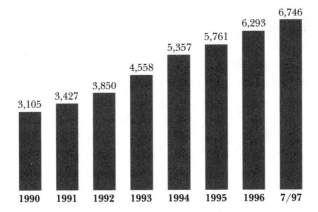

Source: A Guide to Mutual Funds, Investment Company Institute, Washington, D.C.
Reprinted with permission.

FIGURE 6.8 NO-LOAD VERSUS LOAD FUNDS

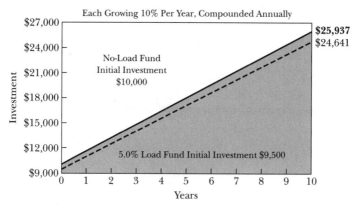

Source: *Investor's Guide to Low-Cost Mutual Funds,* Mutual Fund Education Alliance. Reprinted with permission.

• *Money market funds* are a good place to safely stash some money for the short term.

• *Aggressive stock funds* focus on small companies that are just getting it together. They will require some patience on your part if you hope to see your money grow in any significant fashion. Don't expect any dividends from these fellows.

FIGURE 6.9 INVESTOR'S RISK SPECTRUM

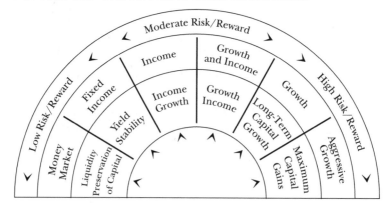

Source: *Investor's Guide to Low-Cost Mutual Funds,* Mutual Fund Education Alliance. Reprinted with permission.

FIGURE 6.10 SERVICES AVAILABLE FROM MUTUAL FUND COMPANIES

	AUTOMATIC INVESTMENT PROGRAM	REDUCED OR WAIVED MINIMUMS FOR AUTO INVESTMENTS	TRANSACTIONS BY TELEPHONE	CHECKING PRIVILEGES (MONEY MARKET ACCOUNTS)	TRANSMISSION OF REDEMPTION PROCEEDS TO BANK ACCOUNT	24-HOUR ACCOUNT ACCESS
American Express Financial Direct	▲		▲	▲		
The Benham Group	▲	▲	▲	▲	▲	▲
Berger Associates, Inc.	▲	▲	▲	▲	▲	▲
The Bramwell Funds, Inc.	▲	▲	▲	▲	▲	▲
Buffalo Group of Funds	▲	▲	▲		▲	
Bull & Bear Funds	▲	▲	▲	▲	▲	
The Dreyfus Family of Funds	▲	▲	▲	▲	▲	
The Fairmont Fund					▲	
Fidelity Investments	▲		▲	▲	▲	▲
Founders Funds	▲	▲	▲	▲	▲	▲
Fremont Mutual Funds	▲		▲		▲	
Gabelli Funds, Inc.	▲	▲	▲	▲	▲	▲

FIGURE 6.10 (CONTINUED)

	AUTOMATIC INVESTMENT PROGRAM	REDUCED OR WAIVED MINIMUMS FOR AUTO INVESTMENTS	TRANSACTIONS BY TELEPHONE	CHECKING PRIVILEGES (MONEY MARKET ACCOUNTS)	TRANSMISSION OF REDEMPTION PROCEEDS TO BANK ACCOUNT	24-HOUR ACCOUNT ACCESS
Heartland Funds	◄	◄	◄	◄	◄	◄
IAI Mutual Funds	◄	◄	◄	◄	◄	◄
INVESCO Funds Group	◄	◄	◄	◄	◄	◄
Janus Funds	◄	◄	◄	◄	◄	◄
Jones & Babson, Inc.	◄	◄	◄	◄	◄	
The Kaufmann Fund, Inc.	◄	◄	◄	◄	◄	
Lexington Group	◄	◄	◄	◄	◄	◄
The Lindner Funds	◄	◄	◄	◄	◄	
Loomis Sayles Funds	◄		◄	◄	◄	
The Montgomery Funds	◄	◄	◄	◄	◄	◄
Payden & Rygel Mutual Funds			◄	◄	◄	
The Reserve Funds	◄		◄	◄	◄	◄
The Royce Funds	◄	◄	◄	◄	◄	◄

FIGURE 6.10 (CONTINUED)

SAFECO Mutual Funds	◀	◀	◀	◀	◀	◀	◀
Charles Schwab & Co., Inc.	◀	◀	◀	◀	◀	◀	◀
Scudder, Stevens & Clark, Inc.	◀	◀	◀	◀	◀	◀	◀
The Selected Funds	◀	◀	◀	◀	◀	◀	◀
Sit Mutual Funds	◀		◀	◀	◀	◀	◀
Stein Roe Mutual Funds	◀	◀	◀	◀	◀	◀	◀
Stratton Management Company	◀	◀	◀		◀		◀
Strong Funds, Inc.	◀	◀	◀	◀	◀	◀	◀
T. Rowe Price Associates, Inc.	◀	◀	◀	◀	◀	◀	◀
Transamerica Investors	◀	◀	◀	◀	◀	◀	◀
Twentieth Century Mutual Funds	◀	◀	◀	◀	◀	◀	◀
USAA Investment Management	◀	◀	◀	◀	◀	◀	◀
U.S. Global Investors, Inc.	◀	◀	◀	◀		◀	◀
The Vanguard Group	◀	◀	◀	◀	◀	◀	◀
Westcore Funds	◀	◀	◀	◀	◀	◀	◀

Source: Investor's Guide to Low-Cost Mutual Funds, Mutual Fund Education Alliance. Reprinted with permission.

FIGURE 6.11 HOW TO READ NEWSPAPER FUND QUOTATIONS

The following is an example of how mutual fund tables appear in many newspapers.

Apzbc:					Gsrxab r	12.96	N.L.	−	.04
Axyte	9.95	10.73	...		Hilt ltd	10.54	N.L.	−	.02
Bxy Xer	10.37	11.33	−	.01	Holpre r	8.40	N.L.	−	.02
Dar Rppe	7.38	8.07	+	.09	Hprl Rd	13.58	N.L.	+	.07
Income	3.16	3.45	+	.01	Nev Sra	16.65	N.L.	−	.01
Tbq Ratl	9.97	10.47	+	.01	Ow Nort	13.53	N.L.	+	.17
Tbqr Dt	10.19	10.70	−	.02	Sys Run	5.08	N.L.	+	.01
Xypr Ap r	10.05	10.98	−	.01	Tqr Hyd	8.73	N.L.	+	.02
Brlkd:					Tuir IS	10.26	N.L.	−	.03
Blgr Dfr	15.64	16.46	−	.03	Tvsa Ei	5.11	N.L.	+	.01
Bmo Pnc	8.54	N.L.	−	.06	Veersl Yr	9.49	9.87	+	.07
Bto Bmd	7.27	7.65	...		Fdrlk:				
Cmyog:					Uhd Eec p	10.18	N.L.	+	.03
MIA p	11.86	12.79	+	.01	Rho Qnd p	10.77	N.L.	+	.02
MIX	11.44	12.33	+	.03	Iro Nico p	8.54	N.L.	−	.06
MIY p	9.70	10.46	−	.01	Gpprl:				
MBF	11.58	12.49	+	.04	Allist B	24.00	N.L.	+	.01
MBI	14.77	15.92	+	.20	Cuy Nihi	10.76	N.L.	−	.03
MBR	11.99	12.93	+	.03	Eqryti	15.87	16.71	+	.02
MRI	13.47	14.18	−	.04	Ginta Ir	12.00	N.L.	+	.01
MII	7.66	8.26	+	.02	Gvrt Lis	10.18	N.L.	+	.03
MDX	10.00	10.50	...		Heai Iec	10.40	10.51	−	.02
DMX r	9.74	10.23	...		Jbd Hld	10.23	10.77	−	.04
GYI	6.93	7.47	−	.03	JiY Sun	14.78	15.40	+	.03
JAM	10.01	10.79	−	.02	Mini JN	10.93	N.L.	−	.01
JEL	10.09	10.59	−	.06	Op Sec	12.97	13.65	...	
MTNC	10.25	10.76	−	.02	Prtn Ta	16.40	17.26	+	.03
MPRS r	10.12	10.62	+	.02	Rsil Nc	15.33	16.14	−	.06
Jellies	20.33	N.L.	+	.01	Esrch R t	9.24	N.L.	−	.04
Sulter	23.81	N.L.	+	.13	Xiil Ndix	12.13	12.77	+	.22
Drxpg:					Htoje:				
Bakc Jau	15.45	16.52	+	.06	ACT trp t	47.99	49.22	+	.06
Cryl Ba	20.68	22.12	+	.05	ACT asp r	48.89	50.14	+	.11
Gryd 3	12.10	12.60	−	.04	Aal AxC	14.15	14.86	−	.03
Frp Dup	9.80	10.45	−	.11	Batl Pd	10.18	N.L.	+	.03
Fye Pm	12.61	N.L.	...		Chrg tt	14.28	15.61	−	.01
Hy Finc	8.19	8.53	−	.01	Dnriy E f	11.04	12.07	+	.03
Hx Papie	10.96	11.42	−	.06	Grante	12.02	13.14	−	.02
Lerl Eiy t	10.02	10.95	+	.02	Hdro le	11.53	12.60	−	.01
Jxt RP	10.90	11.12	−	.04	Ilen Hc	18.82	20.57	+	.12
Lante	12.01	13.14	−	.02	Jl Ncom	11.97	12.84	−	.06
Mina Si	7.36	7.67	−	.01	Kgh Pod p	15.46	16.58	−	.01
MsalT t	9.56	9.96	+	.01	Tbq Ratl	17.07	18.60	+	.08
Nuz Bai	9.85	9.95	...		Tbqr Dt	10.72	11.72	+	.01
Oceana	16.49	17.64	+	.12	Xypr Ap	15.45	16.22	−	.04
Rhoen	11.68	12.49	−	.03	Brlkd:				
Sol Mech	8.89	9.72	+	.10	Blgr Dfr	15.64	16.46	−	.03
Tpx Salu	12.72	13.60	+	.01	Bmo pnc f	8.73	N.L.	+	.02
Urx Chi	6.67	7.39	+	.03	Bto Bmd	7.27	7.65	...	
Urbd Dvr	4.49	5.40	+	.04	MIA	11.86	12.79	+	.01
Grxya	15.30	N.L.	+	.04	MIX	11.44	12.33	+	.03

100

- The first column is the abbreviated fund's name. Several funds listed under a single heading indicate a family of funds.

- The second column is the Net Asset Value (NAV) per share as of the close of the preceding business day. In some newspapers, the NAV is identified as the sell or the bid price—the amount per share you would receive if you sold your shares (less the deferred sales charge, if any). Each mutual fund determines its net asset value every business day by dividing the market value of its total assets, less liabilities, by the number of shares outstanding. On any given day, you can determine the value of your holdings by multiplying the NAV by the number of shares you own.

- The third column is the offering price or, in some papers, the buy or the asked price—the price you would pay if you purchased shares. The buy price is the NAV plus any sales charges. If there are no initial sales charges, an NL for "no-load" appears in this column, and the buy price is the same as the NAV. To figure the sales charge percentage, divide the difference between the NAV and the offering price by the offering price. Here, for instance, the sales charge is 5 percent ($14.18 − $13.47 = $0.71; $0.71 ÷ $14.18 = 0.050).

- The fourth column shows the change, if any, in net asset value from the preceding quotation—in other words, the change over the most recent one-day trading period. This fund, for example, gained six cents per share.

- A "p" following the abbreviated name of the fund denotes a fund that charges an annual fee from assets for marketing and distribution costs, also known as a 12b-1 fee.

- If the fund name is followed by an "r," the fund has either a contingent deferred sales charge (CDSC) or a redemption fee. A CDSC is a charge if shares are sold within a certain period; a redemption fee is a fee applied whenever shares are sold.

- An "f" indicates a fund that habitually enters the previous day's prices instead of the current day's.

- A "t" designates a fund that has both a CDSC or a redemption fee and a 12b-1 fee.

Other footnotes may also apply to a fund listing. Please see the explanatory notes that accompany mutual fund tables in your newspaper.

Source: A Guide to Mutual Funds, Investment Company Institute, Washington, D.C. Reprinted with permission.

- *Balanced mutual funds* are relatively conservative and split their investments between stocks and bonds.

- *Growth mutual funds* offer a bit more security than small-company funds, but they, too, are unlikely to pay any income and are best held for a longer time horizon, say five to seven years.

- *Income funds* invest in income stocks such as utilities. You'll receive dividends here.

- *Growth and income funds* offer a mixture of each. These, too, are for the longer haul.

- *Index funds* mirror indexes like the S & P 500.

- *International funds* are a great way to hedge your bets against the U.S. stock market in these dizzying days of the Dow nipping 8000.

- *Sector funds* invest in just one type of industry (for example, technology companies). Some invest in *cyclical stocks* such as automakers and homebuilders whose profitability depends on the strength of the economy.

- *Bond funds* invest in government bonds, international bonds, and the like.

- *Socially conscious funds* invest only in corporations with stellar environmental records.

The type of fund or mix of funds that you should be considering now will depend in large part on your needs. Do you need current income in order to live? Can you afford to set aside a chunk for the future (riskier types of funds that will have a chance to grow for you)? The point here is that you have to define your objectives. You have already done some preliminary work on this as you clarified your money profile and drew up your budget. One of the best ways to evaluate a given fund is by its performance record.

Buying mutual funds is not difficult. You can either purchase them through a broker or invest directly in the fund
itself. Most funds have 800 numbers you can call to request a
prospectus that gives you the lowdown on the fund's past
record and investment objectives. You then fill out the application and mail it off with a check. There are thousands of
funds today that charge no sales commissions or fees. These
are called *no-load funds* and are generally the funds you are
going to want to buy. (They are the *only* ones I buy.) *Load
funds,* on the other hand, charge sales fees, which can range
anywhere from 1% to 8% of your principal. Typically, funds
bought through a bank or broker are load funds, although
increasingly both banks and brokerages are offering no-load
funds as well.

ASSET ALLOCATION

Getting a read on the types of investment choices open to you
is a first step toward achieving your goals. However, the key to
your success as an investor is knowing how to balance your
portfolio in a manner that lets you grow your money over various time periods and also protect your principal. This is called
asset allocation, and every woman's investment mix will be different. Generally speaking, common stocks have been twice as
profitable as corporate bonds over the past 60 years. Your
investment mix will depend on your age in large measure. If
you are in your 40s and can afford the risk, you might want to
have a third of your portfolio invested in large-company stock
funds, a quarter in small-company funds, another 15% in foreign funds, 20% in bonds or bond funds, and a small amount
in CDs or money market funds. As you grow older, your balance should shift into less-risky investments like T-bills. *Diversification,* or spreading your assets across different types of
investments, will help to mitigate your risk.

Another great way to learn to invest regularly is to consider *dollar cost averaging.* This means that you set aside a specific amount of money from your monthly budget, maybe $200, and arrange to have it automatically invested in a particular mutual fund or public stock. That way you don't have to fret about whether you have timed your investment exactly right. Some months you'll buy high, other months low, and it will all balance out in the end.

You might want to consider an *asset management account,* which is a combination of several types of accounts (for example, a brokerage account, a savings account, and a checking account.)

Of course, there are many other ways you could invest your money. Collectibles such as artworks or coin collections fit into this category. There are real estate investments you can make aside from your primary home. There are large numbers of partnerships in ventures like oil and gas exploration or gold. Although some of these can be wonderfully fun to own and may appreciate over time, they really aren't right for women who are just out on their own in the investing world. Maybe down the road you will be ready to take more chances and have the time to do your homework on some of these opportunities. For now, I'd stick with the basic, straightforward investments that have produced solid returns over time. Keep it simple.

In the next chapter, you'll learn what to do if you and your spouse were involved in a family business.

CHAPTER SEVEN

―――――― $ ――――――

When a Business Is Involved

I t's estimated that about a quarter of a million husband-and-wife teams operate businesses together. These run the gamut from small law firms to antique stores to consulting practices to fast-food franchises. For both widows and divorcing women, knowing how to handle your financial affairs when a business is involved is essential. The reason: Your husband's and/or his and your business could be your most valuable asset, far beyond what your home is worth.

GETTING YOUR SHARE

Regardless of the type of business, a mom-and-pop bike shop or deli, it's essential to know just what that business is worth today and what its future growth is likely to be. You'll also want to be aware of any liabilities or debts the firm may have that you would be responsible for paying back. You must get a handle on these figures as soon as you can bring yourself to focus on the larger financial picture.

Any woman who isn't informed about the inner workings of the family company is setting herself up to be taken advantage of by either her ex-husband, her deceased spouse's partners, or other scavengers. A woman who is naive in matters of business is a conspicuous target for a variety of folks looking to help themselves to the spoils.

For many suddenly single women, a house, an investment portfolio, and maybe jewelry or collectibles come to mind when you think of assets you own, but business interests are not to be overlooked—they can be quite substantial. Sure, there may be other people involved (partners, investors, and the like), but this is one asset you can't afford to ignore. In fact, because of the very nature of its ongoing operation, quickly taking stock is imperative.

If you're going through a divorce, you must have an accurate value of any business interests before your divorce negotiations begin to ensure that you receive an equitable buyout. You'll regret it if you don't take the time to do this.

Separating your personal finances from your spouse's is difficult and tension-filled, and so is disentangling yourself from his business or your joint company. It's also possible that the roles may be reversed and he may be going after a piece of *your* business. Knowing precisely what that asset is worth ahead of time can help you avoid major financial losses. Ignorance can have a walloping negative impact on your bank account. And that's money you will no doubt need to ease the transition into the next stage of your life.

If your spouse is terminally ill, try to get up to speed regarding the business while he is still alive and lucid. Discuss where important papers are located and what he thinks you should do to make it a smooth transition. You need to think hard about your possible future role in the firm. If you're not interested in keeping the company, you'll need to understand your options so you can make wise decisions expeditiously to maximize your asset's value and your future net worth.

Making your way through the financial makeup of the business may seem like a monumental task. Certainly it's a far tougher assignment than getting your personal papers in order. Nonetheless, a business doesn't stop just because your spouse has passed away or you two are splitting up. There are clients to deal with, orders to fill, bills and employees to pay, and much more. It's very possible that you will be called upon in the early days after your spouse's death or departure from your life to make major decisions about the future of the firm as it relates to your own best interests. The employees and other managers are in a state of confusion, as well. No doubt they are worried about the future of the company and their jobs.

DETERMINING THE VALUE OF YOUR BUSINESS

In Chapter 4, you completed a worksheet to help you calculate your net worth and add up your total assets in order to figure out how much money you have on hand. This pool of money is what you have at your disposal to support yourself and family in the days to come. If you are one of those couples who were in business together, or even if one or both of you had your own independent businesses (that is, you didn't work for someone else), the company or companies can represent an enormous amount of money to you.

You may have made a guesstimate about what it all was worth, but now it's time to run the real numbers. Whatever the nature of the business, you'll need to have its value appraised by an unbiased professional. This asset is too important to be appraised by a novice or to try to do it your-self. It's not a guessing matter. It's your future financial health.

Don't panic. You won't have to do the math all by yourself. There are professionals who do these kind of business appraisals for a living. And it's worth paying them for their expertise. I'll tell you how to track down a reputable appraiser. Just be sure you are comfortable with the person you hire and trust that individual. Again, these are apt to be very private, personal financial disclosures.

In a privately held family business, it's not always simple to follow the money trail. There may be outstanding loans that have been done on a handshake alone. The books may not be as neat and up-to-date as they would be for a public com-pany. Needy relatives may be listed as employees even though they don't actually perform much on-site work.

If you are a widow, you may very well want to sell the busi-ness, particularly if you weren't active in its day-to-day affairs. That will present a whole set of separate issues for you. Know-ing what the business is worth, finding a buyer, and negotiat-ing a successful deal will take time and plenty of clear thinking. Having a professional help you will make the process bearable and, hopefully, make it a profitable venture for you as well.

There may be partners involved who would be interested in buying you out. Then again, you might simply want to throw yourself into the business and learn the ropes or, if you have already been working with your husband, decide to take on more and more responsibilities. Either way, you'll need to get the business assets tallied up in order to put together your financial picture, business plan, and invest-ment strategy.

Beyond the money issues involved, there are legal issues that have to be addressed. You have to be hard-nosed about determining the course of action that will best serve *your* interests.

If you are divorcing and trying to track down the value of your spouse's company, be skeptical of anything he passes off to you as "proven documentation" about the financial workings of the firm. There are dozens of wily ways your ex might disguise the company's true value to avoid paying you your fair share. Even if things are amicable on the surface, he has a very personal agenda: to hang onto his business and maximize his advantage.

GETTING AN APPRAISAL

You'll definitely want to hire a professional, usually an accountant, who can plow through the company's books and records to determine the value of the computers and other equipment, the building (if it is owned by the company and not a lease situation), and any additional real estate holdings that might be involved. The appraiser will need to know how much income is generated each year and how that is likely to grow over the next several years. There are also intangibles to take into consideration (for example, how recognizable is the firm's name, and what does this add to its total market worth?).

For widows, don't be duped into accepting your husband's partners' financial rundown of the firm. I know you probably trust these guys and want to leave it to them to keep things going until you have your feet on the ground. Don't. If possible, get an independent evaluation before you even have that first meeting. This will empower you to make wise choices about the dispensation of the company and the role you want to play.

Of course, in the process of divorcing, you can save yourself some money by agreeing to use the same appraiser as your husband—but I'd advise against it. This is one rather large asset for which you should have your own independent appraisal. Even though your husband might be utterly helpful and willing to disclose all on the surface, take a second look.

Certainly in a down and dirty divorce it is not unusual for a husband to try to find ways to disguise a business's true value. He might hide profits or pump up the company's expense statements or even list false employees on the roster. There are a million tricks someone can pull to bury a firm's value, so make sure you hire someone who can do some sleuthing for you as well. Nothing is as it appears on the surface—that's a given.

To have a business appraised, you might be able to find someone trustworthy through your attorney or current accountant. If not, you can call the American Society of Appraisers at 800-272-8258. The Herndon, Virginia–based association can provide you with a list of accredited appraisers in your area.

Figuring out how to divide up the business will depend in large measure on whether the business is in your name, his name, or owned jointly, as well as the state you live in. In most divorce situations, whoever owns the business will not actually sell it, but rather, will substitute another asset (perhaps your house) for the value you are owed.

That's what Claire did, for instance, in order to make sure she held onto her successful landscaping business. Her husband got the house, as you may recall from the introduction. Then her business fell apart. Though unfortunate, she nonetheless thought she had done the right thing by giving him the house rather than a slice of her business. In some cases, though, you might both agree to sell the business outright, split the funds, and move on.

DIVIDING THE SPOILS

Once you know what the business is worth, then you have to figure out how you are going to proceed: whether to sell it, keep it, or in the case of divorce, possibly split it up. The complexity can be astounding, so make sure you have some reliable people on your team to help figure this out. In addition to the appraiser, these helpers might include an accountant and an attorney.

A business is fully regarded as marital property, similar to your home and other investments. If you are living in a community-property state such as Arizona or California, you will be awarded half of all the assets the two of you accumulated during the marriage. If your husband started the company before you were married, it will be a little tougher to determine just how much is owed to you. The same thing goes if you started your firm before you married him. If you began your own business during the marriage, he will have rights to it as well.

In the 40 equitable-distribution states, the business is considered by the courts to be marital property, but don't dream that you are necessarily about to be awarded a full 50% of its worth. In those states, roughly half to two-thirds of your combined assets and incomes will be awarded to the one who earns the most money, and that is probably not going to be you.

Typically, once a divorce is filed, you'll have up to 90 days to file a statement of worth and list all the assets. Don't just blindly trust what your ex's lawyer says the business is worth. The judge will consider a dozen or more other factors before he divides the pie. For example, the amount of time and effort you have put into running and growing the business is an important consideration. The more involved you have been, the more payback you will likely receive. In some states, you can even petition to recoup any education expenses you paid for your ex, such as law school tuition.

Try to get your hands on as much information as you can about the company and all its records. If you can get copies of the tax returns for the last five years or so, that's terrific. Knowledge is money, after all. And if you have been a tidy record keeper, you're probably going to be in good shape. You will need hard-copy proof of any money you put into expanding the firm, so go through your files for canceled checks and other documentation. Finally, if you have any joint accounts, or if both of your names are listed on loan documents, you'll want to write to the applicable institutions and tell them to make no transactions without your approval.

NEGOTIATING THE DEAL

Where a business is involved, your current and future tax situation and financial needs will determine how you make a deal. If other partners are involved, it will complicate things further and require some different financial footwork. If you are a widow, you'll want to meet as soon as possible with your husband's partners to set in motion a course that will allow you access to the firm's records. You and the partners should come to a consensus about how you want (and need) to proceed. Make sure you have your lawyer or appraiser on hand when you do so. This is a trying time for everyone, and you want to be sure you have a representative who can make sense of it all for you and ask the right questions if you feel unprepared.

In a firm with several partners, there is usually a prior pact, known as a *crisscross agreement,* stating that if a partner leaves the firm or dies, the other partners will buy him or her out. In the case of a divorce, the other partners might opt to buy you out or loan your spouse money to do so. Partnerships also might have agreed legally when the firm was formed to valuate the business based on something concrete, like the prior year's profits. A judge might insist on the present-day value, but you can't be sure of that.

Privately owned companies may be tricky enough to figure out, but if the company is public, the process of recouping what you are owed can be even tougher. If you have founder's stock, you'll have to abide by the Securities and Exchange Commission regulations. There could be a six-month waiting period before you can cash out your shares, or you may have to make some public disclosure of your intention to do so well in advance of your actions. Most judges, however, will value your shares at the time you sell, not at the time of the buyout agreement.

WHAT ABOUT TAXES?

Taxes may reduce the amount you receive. (What a surprise.) If stock shares are involved, there is a very real possibility that you will have to pay capital gains tax when the shares are sold. That will happen if the shares have appreciated in value since you first received them.

If stock is not involved, you'll be fine, because you won't be taxed on a straight transfer of cash—*providing* your spouse pays you off within the two-year time frame imposed by the Internal Revenue Service. Any money matters and property transfers not completed within two years of a divorce are considered to be taxable.

If you do find yourself in the position of having to accept a promissory note from your spouse because he doesn't have the resources to pay you off immediately, try to keep the time frame as tight as you can. Also, make sure he has something of value to back up that loan—and not your primary home, thank you. The promissory note needs to include some collateral that will default to you if he can't pay in the agreed-upon time frame.

In Chapter 8, you'll learn how to put your estate plan together. Whether you have been widowed or divorced, properly planning your estate is paramount to maximize your financial security—and your children's if you have any. Estate planning is complicated. It covers everything from writing a will to making sure you have the right amount of life insurance. We'll take a look at what's involved and how you should approach it in a calm and logical fashion.

CHAPTER EIGHT

$

Planning Your Estate

A ny woman on her own should have an *estate plan* pulled together. It doesn't have to be fancy, complicated, or terribly extensive. It all depends on your financial and family situation. But once you've wrangled your way through your husband's estate (either as a result of his death or in trying to divide your assets), you can't neglect to address your own.

Being financially independent means that you are solely responsible for making sure your assets are dispersed according to your wishes when you die and that your heirs won't be stuck paying burdensome taxes on what you leave behind. You're also the one who has to decide what will happen to your children should you no longer be able to care for them. For that, you'll want to choose someone to make decisions concerning your estate, your children, and even your own medical care if you are incapacitated.

CHOOSING YOUR ESTATE ATTORNEY

If you are widowed, you may decide to enlist the attorney who settled your spouse's estate to help you put your plan together. If you don't already have an estate planning attorney, you can write to your state's bar association and ask for a list of estate specialists in your area. Check to see if the expert you select is a member of an estate planning council. Not every area has a council of this type, but should your city have one, you'll find that those professionals with the most estate planning experience are members of it. You can also consult the *Martin-Hubbell Law Directory* at a library. It rates most U.S. attorneys on their ethics. Look for ratings of AV or BV. These are considered to be the top credentials. If you have trouble finding an attorney with whom you are comfortable, you might call Estate Planning Specialists (800-223-9610). For a fee of around $70, they will analyze your situation and make recommendations about estate planning moves.

Now is the right time to review your property. You probably have turned the corner and are no longer just struggling to get from one day to the next. Knitting together your own long-term financial plan is your next goal, and estate planning is an important part of that strategy. To do so, you should pull out your net asset worksheet. The main question to ask yourself is, "How much do I have at this time and to whom do I want to leave it?" Have this information at hand when you sit down with your estate attorney.

Of course, you probably redid your will immediately after the death of your spouse or following your divorce, but you'll want to review it to make certain that what was important to you several months ago still carries the same weight. Your priorities might be somewhat skewed from what they were months ago, and you'll want to make changes in your will to suit those differences.

What does your estate consist of? Simply said, it's the value of assets you leave at the time of your death. This includes insurance policies, investments, retirement funds, your house, and so forth. If you have a beneficiary named already (for example, maybe the assets in your 401(k) plan are assigned to your brother or child), then of course, those funds will go directly to that individual. Without a will, who gets what and when will be the decision of your state courts. My guess is that how the courts would distribute your assets and how you would do so are not at all the same.

Believe it or not, one of the biggest mistakes people make is in not assigning a beneficiary to their various retirement plans or other investments. When you die, those funds will be taxed and distributed by a court-assigned administrator. In the end, your heirs stand to lose what should rightfully be theirs, and your hard-earned money goes to Uncle Sam.

WRITING A WILL

A *will* is a legal document stating how you wish your property to be dispersed following your death. It can be pretty simple. Many people even choose to write their own wills. But although there is no law requiring you to have a lawyer draw up your will, bypassing professional advice is not always wise. Estate laws can be fairly intricate, and making certain that your will is valid and will hold up in court might require a professional review. Most lawyers will charge you by the hour for their time. In general, a basic will can cost anywhere from $50 to $250, and more complicated ones can run to $3,000 or more.

Should you decide to forgo an attorney, you might want to consult *The Complete Will Kit,* 2nd edition, by Jens C. Appel III and F. Bruce Gentry (Wiley, 1996) There are also software packages on the market that sell for under $50. A competent estate attorney can make certain that you don't get anything wrong that can have repercussions for your heirs. You might want to use the software or book to get all your materials in order, then go to your attorney for the final review and approval. No doubt you'll pay less because your estate lawyer has less work to do to draw up the will.

Here are some basic rules for writing a will that will stand up in court.

- First, it must be signed in the presence of at least two and sometimes three witnesses, depending on the laws of the state you live in.

- Don't ask anyone who is a beneficiary of your property to be a witness. That's a real red flag in terms of validity since it is seen as a conflict of interest.

- If you have been divorced, make sure you remove your ex from any beneficiary clauses. You probably can't do this until your divorce decree is final. You certainly want to strike his name from any of your retirement assets or life insurance policies as quickly as you can.

- Your will should clearly state who will inherit what pieces of your property.

- In writing, name the person you have asked to be in charge of making sure your wishes are followed. The person you select to distribute your property is called your *executor.*

- You will have to detail how and when the assets are to be distributed. If you are leaving assets to young children, you might not want them to receive those funds until they reach a certain age; even then, you might want the funds to be paid out at intervals instead of all at once. A *property guardian* is essential, particularly if you have young children, because in most states children under 18 are not considered legally competent to deal with assets or property worth more than a certain amount—sometimes no more than $5,000. Thus, any inheritance left to your children must be managed by an adult until they come of age.

- The property guardian can be the same person as your child's *guardian*. Without a guardian named by you, the court will name one for you and your estate will be divided equally among your children. You should consider naming two separate guardians, one to raise your children and the other to watch over your property. The first person is someone you designate to raise the children in a manner that suits you. The property guardian is someone who is financially savvy and can take charge of handling the money issues. This should be someone who shares your investment philosophy and can preserve your money for your children and their future educational needs. For example, your sister may have a child-rearing philosophy similar to yours, so you'd feel comfortable having her raise your children. However, she may not be a good money manager or have any interest in investing or managing money, so she might not be the best person to ensure the children's future financial needs by preserving the assets you leave to them.

- Your will should contain your full name, the date, the names of your executor, guardians, and beneficiaries, plus special bequests and trust arrangements.

- Since your estate is likely to grow after you have signed your will, it makes sense to divide the assets in terms of percentages rather than straight dollar amounts. In other words, if you have four children, you might instruct that each will inherit 25% of your estate. If you have specific bequests such as leaving an opal necklace to your niece Caitlin, spell it out clearly in a letter of intent attached to your will to prevent misunderstandings that could cause family discord.

Your next step is to sign the original of the will and store it in a safe place. In this case, a safe-deposit box isn't the ideal place because a state will often seal its contents following a death until the taxes have been figured out. Make sure someone close to you knows where your will is and can find it easily. You may already be aware of the havoc caused by a missing will if your spouse died without one or you were unable to locate it quickly. Your lawyer might be willing to keep a signed copy in his or her office.

Your will should be reviewed at regular intervals, maybe every two years, to stay current with your life situation. You should definitely consider making adjustments if there are changes in the tax laws or if you move to another state or remarry.

LIVING WILLS

A *living will* is a sort of hybrid will that outlines the kind of medical care you want if you are terminally ill. For example, if you don't want to be kept alive on life support systems, you can make that known. (As morbid as it may seem, this could save your family a substantial sum in medical bills.) In a living will, you can include instructions for organ donation if you wish, and you can designate the person you want to make any medical decisions relating to your care if you are unable to do so.

For a living will to be valid, it must be witnessed by two adults, and they can't be members of your family or medical physicians. You will want to have the document in writing and have it signed and dated. You can call Choice in Dying, a right-to-die advocacy organization, at 800-989-9455, or write to them at 200 Varick Street, New York, NY 10013, to get the necessary forms to draft a living will and obtain advice about how the laws work in your state.

DURABLE POWER OF ATTORNEY

A *durable power of attorney* for health care, or *health care proxy*, is a good supplement to a living will. It permits you to name someone to make financial and health care decisions for you if you are incapacitated in some way (say, in a coma) but still alive. Your designee can sign checks to pay your bills.

There is no reason you can't have both a living will and a durable power of attorney, and, in fact, you probably should have both. Typically, you would ask a friend or close relative to take on this responsibility. But be sure you have discussed it with them and that they have agreed to do so ahead of time. Many financial advisors recommend that you have two people designated as powers of attorney, one for medical purposes and one for financial matters. Most states recognize these wills, but the legalities can vary. Make sure your doctors and people you pick as your proxies have a copy of the will. As with a living will, the document must be signed, dated, notarized, and witnessed by at least one adult. It should cost you about $100 to have your attorney draw up a power of attorney document for you.

NAMING AN EXECUTOR

When you write your will, you will name an executor of your estate to make sure dispersement of your assets is carried out according to your wishes. Your executor is responsible for paying debts and distributing what is not already assigned to a beneficiary. Your life insurance policies and retirement plans have probably already been directed to a certain individual.

An executor normally is paid a fee of 3% to 5% of your total estate. Sometimes, if this person is someone close to you, he or she may opt to pass on the fee. To assign a value to your property, your executor might have to hire an accountant or other professional. Again, make sure the person you name is someone who is willing to take on the task, which can entail a fair amount of time and effort and be emotionally taxing.

TRUSTS TO CONSIDER

A *living trust* is something you might consider establishing for yourself. You will want to consult an estate planning attorney in order to get the best advice on how to structure a living trust. Basically, you name yourself as the trustee of the trust and designate someone else, maybe your lawyer, as your successor to administer the trust should you become incapacitated because of an illness or accident.

The trust takes effect immediately, and it can be *revocable*, meaning changes are allowed at any time, or *irrevocable*, meaning no changes allowed. Basically, with a revocable trust you can retain control. The key advantage is that when you die your heirs receive the assets without having to go through *probate*, which is the legal process that a court requires to determine if a will is valid and to make sure your property is distributed properly. Probate, believe it or not, can take up to two years for your heirs to battle through and can lop off as much as 10% of your estate assets in fees. Unlike probated estates, property that is part of a trust is not a matter of public record when you die; no one can find out what you left to whom, and private matters will stay that way.

To execute a living trust, you will have to rename all of your assets in the trust name (for example, the Becky Hackel Trust). The assets that you are renaming will include everything from your savings accounts to any mutual funds you hold.

It's not hard to do this; it just takes a bit of time. You have to write to your bank, mutual fund company, and stockbroker and explain what you are doing. Send the first and last pages of the trust papers and the section that says who has trustee rights. In most cases, you will name yourself, but if you really don't want to worry about financial matters because you are ill or are entangled in some other life crisis, you can name someone else to manage your investments for you.

This doesn't mean you give that person absolute power to invest your money without consulting you. You can outline the exact boundaries of responsibility. The point is that this will be a new account in the trust name, not yours, and you will control it in the same manner you did previously. It's very important to retitle all of your assets in the trust name if you want it to hold up in court.

Once you choose to have a living will, you should consider having your attorney attach a *pour-over will,* which allows you to address other matters, such as naming a guardian for your children and designating who should get what in terms of physical possessions.

NAMING A TRUSTEE

You need to name someone to be the trustee of your trust when you die. Since this is a job that may take more than a year or two and is all about money, you should pick someone with expertise in the field of finance and money management. Because this can be a complicated and long-term project, you might want to hammer out a deal with a bank's trust department or an investment firm to manage this service. Typically, they will charge an annual fee of up to 1.5% of the value of the assets under their management.

It's important to divulge your estate plan to a friend or close relative. Your attorney may be tops, but someone closer to you needs to understand what you have in mind. That way, if someone contests the will, there will be an advocate to fight for your wishes. Make sure this individual knows where you have filed your will and whom to call (your lawyer, perhaps) if there is a crisis.

In Chapter 9, you'll learn the ins and outs of investing on-line and taking control of your own investments.

CHAPTER NINE

$

On-Line Investing

C lose to half of all households in this country now have personal computers. Those of you who are computer savvy, or are interested in learning how to be, will find that using the computer to get investment information will save you time and money. Best of all, you can invest from the privacy of your own home—even at 3 A.M. if you so desire.

GREAT WEB SITES

The amount of financial information now available at the click of a mouse is staggering—everything from SEC and mutual fund filings to NASD actions against rogue brokers to stock quotes. And the sheer number of offerings is growing wildly each month.

Large discount brokers like Charles Schwab estimate that by the year 2000 some 40% of all investment trades will be placed via the Internet. At Schwab, about one-quarter of all trades are now taken over the computer. By the year 2000, when 50 million people worldwide will have Net access from home (up from 11 million now), the Web will be the first choice as a source of investment information, so predicts Forrester Research, a Cambridge, Massachusetts, Net watcher.

Using your computer to obtain information about everything from mutual fund performances to determining how much you need to save for retirement can make investing and managing your money simpler and faster. In the last year, the number of electronic, do-it-yourself brokerages has exploded, along with a virtual treasure trove of investing resources both on the Internet and through on-line services like America Online, CompuServe, and Prodigy. You can now tap into instant stock quotes, security analysts' earnings estimates, Morningstar analyst reports, and much much more.

All told, there are about two dozen brokers who will handle your accounts via the Net, the on-line services, or their own proprietary software. On the Internet itself, some dozen firms, including AccuTrade, Charles Schwab, and Discover Brokerage, offer you the chance to trade no-load mutual funds and securities without going through a broker. The number of on-line trading accounts should hit 10 million by 2001, according to Forrester, up from 600,000 in 1995. And individuals are expected to manage around $525 million through on-line accounts by the century's end, up from about $100 million in 1997. (See Figure 9.1.)

The quality of Net offerings ranges from not-worth-the-bother to superb. Plenty of sites offer little more than a mutual fund manager's photo and past-performance figures. But many are gold mines for investors, with up to a thousand pages of information. Recently, some organizations have launched sites aimed exclusively at women and money issues. In the fall of 1997, Hearst New Media and Technology (http://www.homearts.com), for example, began offering women's personal finance materials and articles relating to women and money on its home page.

FIGURE 9.1 HOW ON-LINE INVESTING IS GROWING

YEAR	NUMBER OF ACCOUNTS (IN MILLIONS)
1995	0.6
1996	1.5
1997	2.77
1998	5.11
1999	6.87
2000	8.45
2001	10.05

Source: Forrester Research

MUTUAL FUNDS ON-LINE

With a few clicks of a mouse, you can scroll through performance data on thousands of mutual funds, screen for a list of choices that are suitable for you, download prospectuses and applications, and print them out. You may just want to check out your fund family's home page, but there's so much more to choose from.

Some of the best sites are Calvert Group, Fidelity Investment's Online Investor Center, Gabelli, T. Rowe Price, and Vanguard. In general, they offer basic investment education and extensive fund information. They also serve up interactive retirement planning and college-savings worksheets. They can help you select an investment strategy based on your own financial objectives, and they make it easy for you to identify the funds that would be best for you given your criteria and investment goals. If you are intimidated about firing up your computer and jumping straight to the Web, you might pick up a guide book such as *Mutual Funds on the Net: Making Money Online* by Paul B. Farrell (John Wiley & Sons) and *Mutual Fund Investing on the Internet* by Peter G. Crane (AP Professional) that can give you a solid overview of what is available and the pertinent addresses.

An excellent starting point, particularly for mutual fund investors, is Intuit's Quicken site. This site is an investment cybermall of sorts, providing Morningstar reports on over 6,500 funds and 8,000 stocks that can be screened according to your criteria. You can get price quotes, investment advice, and links to 1,000-plus sites of public companies. Invest-o-rama is another good Net home page that is loaded with links to mutual fund companies and much more.

Another top place is Morningstar's own site. In reality, it is probably the best source of mutual fund information currently available on the Net, giving you access to Morningstar's entire database of nearly 8,000 funds and about 8,000 stocks. You will find prices updated daily and up to 10 years of performance records. You can get all the data about a fund's fees, its risk classification, and its breakdown by sector (such as technology). You can also peruse a company's balance sheets for the past two years and get the latest financial news.

One of the most unique features of the site is something called X-Ray View. You plug in the ticker symbol for all the funds you own and the total value of each holding, and X-Ray View then adds up all the stocks and bonds in each of your funds and generates a pie chart showing your true asset allocation. You might think your funds are invested only in stocks when in reality your money is also invested in bonds or cash. Managers do make changes, sometimes on a daily basis, but X-Ray View will give you a good snapshot of your holdings at a particular point in time.

The American Association of Individual Investors, too, has a weighty amount of material on mutual fund topics and reviews investing software as well as offering basic information on how to invest by computer.

Here are some investing sites worth visiting:

Calvert Group: http://www.calvertgroup.com

Charles Schwab: http://www.schwab.com

Fidelity Investments: http://www.fidelity.com

Gabelli Funds: http://www.gabelli.com

Invest-o-rama: http://www.investorama.com

Morningstar: http://www.morningstar.net

Mutual Funds Magazine: http://www.mfmag.com

The American Association of Individual Investors:
  http://www.aaii.org

The Vanguard Group: http://www.vanguard.com

T. Rowe Price: http://www.troweprice.com

ON-LINE TRADING

On-line trading is appealing because it's cheap and easy. Setting up an account is no different than opening any other kind of brokerage account. You fill out an application that you can download from the broker's Web site and mail in a minimum balance of, say, $1,000 to $5,000 to activate the account. Once your check clears, you're sent a password, an account number, and a private ID user code. Commissions range from under $10 to $40 to trade up to 1,000 shares. That's 60% to 80% less than you would pay a discount broker.

Buy 100 shares at $40 apiece through Schwab's electronic brokerage and you'll pay $29.95 in commissions. Order the same amount through a Schwab broker and you'll pay $55.

And those commissions are rapidly decreasing. You will, however, have the cost of Internet access, which might average $20 a month depending on your service provider.

There are some drawbacks, of course. For example, it's difficult to get a real person on the phone if you have a problem. Some brokers require you to contact them only through e-mail. Others permit one call a month. And you might be charged extra if you request a stock certificate or trade fewer than five times a year.

Here's a selection of on-line brokers you might consider.

AccuTrade: http://www.accutrade.com

American Express InvestDirect/pt:
   http://www.Americanexpress.com

Discover Brokerage Direct:
   http://www.discoverbrokerage.com

DLJ Direct: http://www.dljdirect.com

e.Schwab: http://www.schwab.com

E*Trade Securities: http://www.etrade.com

Jack White & Co.: http://www.jackwhiteco.com

Quick & Reilly: http://www.quick-reilly.com

There are many other informative sites for investors. Beside those listed here, you'll no doubt find others you like, and more are being added all the time.

FinanCenter is a site that offers interactive calculators on everything from retirement planning to whether you should buy or lease a car. It can calculate how your monthly expenses will likely change in retirement and what your budget might look like in a pie chart form. There are 10 areas ranging from budgeting to saving to credit cards and retirement planning. Clicking on a question such as "Am I saving enough each month to retire at age 65?" leads you to a financial calculator geared to helping you understand your financial situation and how you can meet your goals.

Daily Stocks is a site packed with information on thousands of stocks and other links. For example, if you type in "The Gap" you'll get a list of Web sites related to that company's stock, including a link to its home page. You can link to sites that will give you analysts' earnings estimates, dividend information, the company history and profile, as well as news stories from a variety of media outlets, including Reuters and Forbes.

To do some detailed research on a public company, you'll want to go to the Securities and Exchange Commission site. It contains a wealth of information about public companies. The offerings include all filings with the SEC—from annual and quarterly financial reports to prospectuses. Even better, it's all free.

You can run a check on your broker at the National Association of Securities Dealers site to find out if there have been any complaints lodged against him or her.

If you are doing some planning for your golden years, you will find that Quicken's Web site is another good place to look for that kind of advice. It offers a retirement calculator that allows you to plug in a range of variables, from your age to income level and years to retirement, to determine if you are on track for a comfortable retirement. Another government agency that offers insight into your potential retirement funds is the Social Security Administration. At this site, you can request a Personal Earnings and Benefit Estimate Statement, which will estimate your Social Security retirement payout.

To keep tabs on your overall investment portfolio, you might log on to Microsoft Investor. You can track your investments by typing in all your holdings, from mutual funds to stocks and Microsoft Investor will update prices with a click. It can also show you if your stock is near its year high or is getting risky enough to consider selling.

There are literally dozens of Web sites that provide access to stock quotes, including PC Quote, StockMaster, and Yahoo!Finance. Most of the free services, however, do have 15- or 20-minute price delays. The search engine Yahoo! goes a step further and connects you to dozens of other financial sites. There are also many financial publications available online, including *Business Week, Forbes, USA Today, Money,* and *Bloomberg News.*

For those of you who are still nervous about venturing onto the Web, you can pay a monthly fee of up to $20 or hourly fee of around $2.95 to log on to America Online, CompuServe, and Prodigy. Each offers rich resources for individual investors. They are easy to access and quite comprehendible. You'll find stock quotes, company profiles, investment news, and more. You may also chat with other investors and tap into investment forums like AOL's irreverent and informative Motley Fool, hosted by brothers David and Tom Gardner.

While these forums and Net chat groups can be great places to trade information about various investments and find out what other people are doing, be careful about following any tips you get. You must be leery of on-line chat rooms where shady operators hype lousy and sometimes imaginary investments. The SEC is starting to crack down on these operators, but the opportunity for fraud does exist. Shares of stocks have been known to jump from under 20 cents to over $4 and back to under 20 cents within a few months due to these tactics. Always do your own research before making an investment decision.

DUELING PERSONAL FINANCE SOFTWARE

Personal finance software is another helpful way to learn to put together your household budget, pay bills, and track your spending, among other things. Instead of the tedious, time-consuming process of typing in transactions for every receipt, account deposit or withdrawal, and check, you can usually automatically download much of the information directly from your credit card company or bank by accessing the World Wide Web if the software maker has a relationship with the financial institution.

The two biggest players in the field are Quicken from Intuit and Microsoft Money. Quicken, which has been around for more than 13 years, is the undisputed leader, with more than 80% of the retail market, or more than 10 million active users. Since 1992, Microsoft has been trying to overtake the market, but is still playing second fiddle to Quicken.

Both companies sell several variations of the product, with varying degrees of sophistication, features, and yes, prices. In my opinion, Quicken is still the easier of the two programs to navigate. It's faster, cheaper, and offers a broader range of financial planning help (for example, letting users shop for insurance and mortgages via the World Wide Web). Also, you can run it on Macintosh, NT4, Windows 95, and Windows 3.1. To run Money, you'll need Windows 95 or a PC with Windows 95 or NT. Nonetheless, Microsoft's top-of-the-line Microsoft Money 98 Financial Suite does have some highlights worth noting. In general, you probably don't need to spring for Quicken's full-blown package, Quicken Suite 98, at least initially. You may want to upgrade down the road, but its Quicken Deluxe 98 contains most of the functions you will find useful. In regard to Microsoft, its latest Financial Suite has far more useful functions to offer than the basic program, but you'll pay for those extras. Either way, for those of you who are at ease with computing, financial software can make it easy to get organized and to track where you are headed.

MICROSOFT MONEY

Here's what Microsoft Money has to offer:

MICROSOFT MONEY 98

- This is the basic software program that performs fundamental tasks. It sells for around $29.95. Existing Money users and users of Quicken are eligible for a $10 upgrade rebate.

- You can track expenses.

- You can create a budget.

- It creates customized charts and reports so that you can see where your money is going.

- You can track your investment accounts and follow the performance by downloading brokerage statements if your brokerage connects to Money.

- You can bank on-line from over 100 financial institutions. That means you can pay bills electronically. An on-screen bill reminder will alert you when bills are due.

- You can download your bank statements and transfer money between accounts, providing your bank has a relationship with Money.

- Quicken files can be converted in minutes.

MICROSOFT MONEY 98 FINANCIAL SUITE

- This is the version with all the hoopla. You get all the features of Money 98—bill paying, budgeting, and banking services, plus easy conversion from Quicken, and much more.

- Its Goal Planner feature lets you set up short- and-long-term financial goals and easily refine those goals whenever the spirit moves you.

- It links all of your accounts, investments, bills, budget and debt-reduction plans, and automatically shows you an updated view of your finances everytime you log on.

- The Microsoft Investor feature lets you track your portfolio, research detailed data on 8,000 equities and mutual funds, access analyst reports and recommendations, earnings estimates, and stock prices (delayed 20 minutes), including earnings per share and price-to-earnings ratios.

- It allows you to trade on-line through several leading brokerages such as Charles Schwab & Co., E*Trade, and Fidelity Investments. It will also e-mail stock market alerts should the market zigzig impact your portfolio. Your cost: $9.95 a month, or $6.95 if you subscribe to Microsoft Network.

- The Money Insider feature offers basic articles on how to buy insurance, plan for retirement, and the like. Information is updated each time you go on-line. You can also read articles by personal finance experts and peruse a database of frequently asked personal finance questions and answers.

- A feature called Advisor FYI aims to customize incoming Internet information that could impact your individual financial situation. For example, it alerts you when mortgage rates drop and determines whether you are a good candidate for refinancing based on the data you have already provided about your current mortgage.

- There is also a directory of more than 625 fee-only financial planners, indexed by geographical location, provided by the National Association of Personal Financial Advisors.

- Each month the program will generate a report that lists your total spending compared to your budget, and it updates your investment portfolio with the latest valuations.

- Microsoft has signed up over 100 banks, brokers, and credit card issuers—nearly double the number of Quicken.

- Your cost: around $55. Existing Money users get a $15 upgrade rebate, as do Quicken users who switch over.

QUICKEN

Here's what Quicken has to offer:

QUICKEN BASIC

- Nothing fancy here—just a surprisingly simple way to manage daily finances. This is your basic electronic checkbook that allows you to pay bills, track your bank and credit card accounts, receive bills on-line, balance your checkbook, and bank on-line with financial institutions that have agreements with Intuit, such as Citibank, First Chicago, and Wells Fargo.

- There is a reminders' window that displays automatically when you have upcoming bills to pay or your account balance is nearing its minimum.

- You can create a budget and track loans.

- You can dissect your paycheck information so that your income, taxes, 401(k) contributions, and medical contributions are tracked automatically.

- You can easily convert Microsoft Money data files into Quicken data files.

- Your cost for Quicken Basic 98: $39.95 minus a $10 rebate for upgraders.

QUICKEN DELUXE 98

- It offers everything that the basic program does and then some.

- You can access free stock and mutual fund quotes taken from Quicken.com. You can also tap into the latest Morningstar ratings and pore through prospectuses of more than 7,500 mutual funds free of charge.

- Financial news is fed through Reuters.

- The Portfolio View feature lets you analyze your stock and fund performances.

- The program earmarks potential tax deductions.

- It contains an emergency storage place to stash important medical and financial data such as bank account and PIN numbers, the location of safe deposit keys and boxes, and names of doctors and professional advisors.

- You can also shop for auto, life, and other insurance policies through Intuit's InsureMarket site on the Web and compare policies and quotes offered by firms such as All State and Travelers.

- You can also compare national and regional mortgage rates though the QuickenMortgage site on the Web.

- You can bank and trade on-line via Web site links in Quicken if the institution has a relationship with Intuit such as Accutrade, American Express, E*Trade, or Charles Schwab & Co.

- Your cost: $59.95 with a $20 rebate for upgraders.

QUICKEN HOME & BUSINESS 98

- It offers everything packaged in Deluxe.

- You can generate invoices with your own logo and include information that applies to your individual business.

- You can track receivables.

- You can track sales taxes.

- You can track reimbursable expenses.

- You can generate tax reports.

- It automatically calculates state taxes to be collected.

- Your cost: $89.95 with $20 rebate for upgraders.

- This is not available for Macintosh users.

QUICKEN SUITE 98

- This program offers all the bells and whistles of Deluxe 98.

- In addition, there is a Quicken Financial Planner 3.0 section and Quicken Lawyer Deluxe.

- This is not available for Macintosh users.

- You can prepare some 88 legal documents, from a bill of sale for a car to a prenuptial agreement to a living will.

- There's a question-and-answer section that deals with a whole range of legal issues, from disputes with neighbors to how to fix an inaccurate credit rating.

- It can help you put together an estate plan.

- There's a legal dictionary with over 6,500 legal terms.

- Quicken Financial Planner helps you calculate what you will need to retire comfortably and how much it will cost you to send your kids to college.

- You can create a short-range financial plan in as little as 15 minutes or spend hours honing a thorough long-term plan.

- You can calculate whether you have enough life insurance, whether you have enough money to buy a house, and how your assets should be allocated

- Your cost: $89.95 minus $20 upgrade rebate.

Here are more useful addresses for your files:

Business Week: http://www.businessweek.com

Daily Stocks: http://www.dailystocks.com

FinanCenter: http://www.financenter.com

Microsoft Investor: http://www.investor.msn.com

National Association of Securities Dealers:
  http://www.nasdr.com

PC Quote: http://www.pcquote.com

Quicken: http://www.quicken.com

Securities and Exchange Commission: http://www.sec.gov

Social Security Administration: http://www.ssa.gov

StockMaster: http://www.stockmaster.com

Yahoo!Finance: http://www.yahoo.com

Trust me, you don't have to be a sophisticated investor to take advantage of the reams of personal finance and investing material now available on the Internet and through the on-line services. Nor does your PC necessarily have to replace your broker. I do tons of research on-line, for example, but have never felt confident enough to place a trade there, although I'm getting braver every day. However, I do love to keep track of my mutual fund portfolio, researching new funds to buy and making sure my asset allocation is in balance.

The bonanza on the Net is not to be missed if you are serious about learning to invest and manage your money wisely. The offerings are plentiful, and you don't have to be a pro to use it as an investing tool. Just look at it as a huge resource of useful information that's available to help you make tough and tricky investing decisions. Chapter 10 will discuss things you can do to help navigate your way through your financial world should you remarry.

CHAPTER TEN

$

Moving On

Even though you are a single woman today, chances are good that you will find another partner. In fact, divorced women typically remarry within about four to six years, and widows have been known to hook up with a significant other even sooner. Certainly there is nothing wrong with moving on with your life. Wanting to have someone to share with is natural. For many women, that new partner has also been divorced or widowed. Many widows find new mates through a surviving spouse's support group—the companionship and shared experience of grief forms a strong bond.

When you are emotionally ready to consider remarriage, however, there are important money issues to consider. You have worked so hard to establish your own financial identity and to learn to manage your money solo that it's critical to look out for your own financial independence. As unromantic as it may seem, even the most loving marriages include a lot more than hearts and roses. Marriage is at its very roots a financial partnership. The best marriages are about sharing and love, but they are also a money partnership. If you want to save yourself heartbreak and financial loss should your next marriage end in divorce or widowhood, it should be treated as an equal financial partnership from the start.

You can't risk losing the money left to you by your late husband or your divorce settlement by plunging carelessly into a starry-eyed relationship. You don't have to have the treasure chest of an Ivana Trump or Elizabeth Taylor to opt for a *prenuptial agreement.* Separating your emotions from your money is a key factor in protecting yourself against disaster. Years ago it was unheard of to discuss the indelicate topic of money before that stroll down the aisle. Signing a prenuptial agreement seemed to say that you didn't trust your future partner or that you weren't really in it for the long haul. But those days are over. It's no longer insulting to talk about money before you say "I do." It's just plain smart.

WHAT IS A PRENUP?

Simply put, a prenup is a document or pact signed before your marriage that spells out how your assets will be divided in the event of death or divorce. Some people even use it as a plan for how all finances will be managed during their marriage. Some agreements go as far as to require that the husband or wife maintain a regular sexual relationship with the other partner in order to be eligible for any portion of assets. Anything goes. But the important thing is that you discuss your financial lives openly before you remarry. If the man you are planning to marry has been married before or widowed, he may have children to rear. He may also have debts you know nothing about. You need to decide how you want to share your two sets of assets.

There is no need to feel obligated to join your financial lives together in a formal manner. Most financial advisors argue that mingling assets by including your new husband on the title of your house or making or by adding his name to your investments can lead to nothing but trouble, particulary if the man has fewer assets than you do. To ensure that your hard-earned financial stability holds firm, it's advisable to sign a prenup.

The idea of signing a marriage agreement that concerns financial matters isn't new at all. Jewish marriage ceremonies have included the act of signing the ketubah for centuries. The ketubah is a Hebrew pact that defines a husband's obligations to his bride. It covers everything from providing clothes and food to sexual relations. It also states that the husband is responsible for providing a set amount of money for his wife should he leave her through divorce or death.

Writing a prenuptial agreement might cost you a few thousand dollars depending on how complicated it is, but it is a step worth taking for most women marrying for the second time. The agreement can't cover issues related to children, such as child support or custody, but the contract can protect your other assets and even determine who will get custody of your labrador retriever.

HOW TO MAKE A PRENUP HOLD UP IN COURT

The key to making these agreements successful is to begin by each of you hiring your own lawyer. There are thousands of attorneys who specialize in matrimonial law and handle prenups frequently. You don't want your new spouse to be able to argue that there was any type of conflict of interest.

Both you and your future spouse must divulge detailed financial information, including all assets, income, and debts. Full disclosure is paramount. Then the pact must be signed voluntarily by both of you and far enough in advance of your wedding day so your husband can't claim he signed under duress. Two or three months ahead of your wedding date is advisable. And it's probably a good idea to videotape the signing so you have a record. If there are bad feelings about signing a prenup, you might consider setting a future date on which the contract will expire.

WHO NEEDS A PRENUP?

- A woman who is bringing a lot of assets to the partnership ($100,000 and up)
- A woman who has children from a prior marriage
- A woman who owns her own business or is a partner in a company
- A woman on a fast career path who is likely to earn a hefty salary
- A woman who is paying for her spouse to get an advanced degree

POSTNUPTIAL AGREEMENTS

If you don't have a prenup and can't come to an agreement with your ex-spouse during the divorce proceedings, your state laws will dictate division of the assets. That means that in community-property states—Arizona, California, Idaho, Louisiana, Nevada, New Mexico, Texas, Washington, and Wisconsin—you will probably get half of everything. In other states, assets will be split by the court depending on factors such as how long you were married and what you actually accumulated together.

It's never too late to draw up an agreement, even after you have been married for a while. A *postnuptial agreement* is just as valid as a prenup and is set up the same way. You should seriously consider this option if you inherit a lump sum of money or have a large cash infusion from selling a business.

These agreements will hold up in court if they are written properly. Never lose sight of your goal: keeping your financial independence. If the man you want to marry is unwilling to sign an agreement, you should probably take some time to think things through.

Be pragmatic when it comes to linking your life to a new person. Living happily ever after doesn't always happen for most of us. You've learned that the hard way. It takes time to recover from the loss of a spouse, so take it slowly and be honest with yourself. But never forget that being responsible for your own finances and striving to constantly educate yourself about money issues will give you the confidence and freedom to survive these life-shattering blows. Taking control of your financial life is a necessity.

With your financial plan firmly in place, handling money will become a routine part of your daily life. The most difficult work is behind you. You'll want to make a habit of checking up on your investments every six months or so to make sure everything is still on track. Nobody ever said life was fair, but being fiscally fit will make your future brighter.

APPENDIX A

$

Will Planning/ Review Checklist

Use this checklist either to plan a new will or to review an existing will.

CURRENT STATUS				
YES	NO	UNSURE	N/A	
☐	☐	☐	☐	1. If there is an existing will, does it reflect the current situation, including birth of heirs and changes in the tax laws, and not contain obsolete sections, including state or residence and inappropriate selection?
☐	☐	☐	☐	2. Will any specific bequests or legacies be made?
☐	☐	☐	☐	3. Are there any bequests to charity, either outright or in trust?
☐	☐	☐	☐	4. Has the disposition of personal property—furniture, jewelry, and automobiles, for example—been planned?
☐	☐	☐	☐	5. Has provision been made for the disposition of real estate?

		CURRENT STATUS		
YES	**NO**	**UNSURE**	**N/A**	
☐	☐	☐	☐	6. Does the will provide for the disposition of property if an heir predeceases you?
☐	☐	☐	☐	7. Will trusts be established for certain beneficiaries, or will they receive the assets outright?
☐	☐	☐	☐	8. Will certain beneficiaries be provided with periodic payments of income?
☐	☐	☐	☐	9. Does the will take advantage of the unlimited marital deduction to the most effective and practical extent allowed?
☐	☐	☐	☐	10. Has consideration been given to providing for marital and nonmarital trusts in the will?
☐	☐	☐	☐	11. Is the custody of minors satisfactorily addressed?
☐	☐	☐	☐	12. Has consideration been given to appointing a "financial" guardian for the children in addition to a personal guardian?
☐	☐	☐	☐	13. Does the will specify that any minor beneficiary's share of the estate will be held until he or she reaches maturity?
☐	☐	☐	☐	14. Does the will provide for a guardianship or trust to protect the inheritance of disabled or incompetent beneficiaries?
☐	☐	☐	☐	15. Have provisions been made to dispose of business interests?
☐	☐	☐	☐	16. Have appropriate and capable persons or institutions been appointed to serve as executor, trustee, and/or guardian?
☐	☐	☐	☐	17. Does the will name an alternate or successor executor, trustee, and/or guardian?

YES	NO	**CURRENT STATUS** UNSURE	N/A	
☐	☐	☐	☐	18. Should any special powers be given to or taken away from the executor?
☐	☐	☐	☐	19. Has the executor's bond requirement been waived?
☐	☐	☐	☐	20. Are specific powers granted to the executor, as necessary, such as to retain or sell property, to invest trust and estate assets, to allocate receipts and disbursements to income and principal, to make loans and borrow funds, or to settle claims?
☐	☐	☐	☐	21. Is the ownership of the assets complementary to the provisions of the will (i.e., some assets may pass outside of the will by contract or by type of ownership)?
☐	☐	☐	☐	22. Does the will state who will receive property if the beneficiary disclaims it? (Disclaimers can be an effective postmortem planning device.)
☐	☐	☐	☐	23. Have any special directions for the funeral or memorial been provided?
☐	☐	☐	☐	24. Have sources been identified from which debts, funeral expenses, and estate administrative costs will be paid?
☐	☐	☐	☐	25. Will the survivors have enough cash to pay ordinary family living expenses while the estate is in probate?

$

Letter of Instructions Checklist

A letter of instructions is not a legal document like a will. You have a lot more leeway in both the language and content. Your letter is a good place to put personal wishes and final comments, but your heirs will be very grateful if you include details about important financial matters.

☐ First Things to Do
- Acquaintances and organizations to be called, including Social Security, the bank, and your employer
- Arrangements to be made with funeral home
- Lawyer's name and telephone number
- Newspapers to receive obituary information
- Location of insurance policies

☐ Cemetery and Funeral
- Details of your wishes and any arrangements you have made

☐ Facts for Funeral Director
- Vital statistics, including your full name, residence, marital status, spouse's name, date of birth, birthplace,

father's and mother's names and birthplaces, length of residence in state and in United States, military records/history, Social Security number, occupation, and life insurance information

☐ Information for Death Certificate and Filing for Benefits

- Citizen of, race, marital status, name of next of kin (other than spouse), relationship, address, and birthplace

☐ Expected Death Benefits

- Information about any potential death benefits from your employer (including life insurance, profit sharing, pension plan, or accident insurance), life insurance companies, Social Security, the Veterans Administration, or any other source

☐ Special Wishes

- Anything you want them to know

☐ Personal Effects

- A list of who is to receive certain personal effects, usually including details of who is to receive items such as golf clubs or some other special item and it could include autos, etc., in some states

☐ Personal Papers

- Locations of important personal documents, including your will, birth and baptismal certificates, communion and confirmation certificates, diplomas, marriage certificate, military records, naturalization papers, and any other documents (e.g., adoption, divorce)

☐ Safe-Deposit Box*

- Location and number of box and key and an inventory of contents

*State law may require a bank to seal the deceased's safe-deposit box as soon as notified of his or her death, even if the box is jointly owned.

☐ Post Office Box

- Location and number of box and key (or combination)

☐ Income Tax Returns

- Location of all previous returns
- Location of your estimated tax file
- Tax preparer's name

☐ Loans Outstanding

- Information for loans other than mortgages, including bank name and address, name on loan, account number, monthly payment, location of papers and payment book, collateral, and information on any life insurance on the loan

☐ Debts Owed to the Estate

- Debtor, description, terms, balance, location of documents, and comments on loan status/discharge

☐ Social Security

- Full name, Social Security number, and the location of Social Security cards

☐ Life Insurance

- Policy numbers and amounts, location of policy, whose life is insured, insurer's name and address, kind of policy, beneficiaries, issue and maturity date, payment options, and any special facts

☐ Veterans Administration

- If you are a veteran, give information on collecting benefits from local Veterans Administration office

☐ Other Insurance

- If any other insurance benefits or policies are in force, including accident, homeowners/renters, automobile, disability, medical, personal, or professional liability, give insurer's name and address, policy number, beneficiary, coverage, location of policy, term, how acquired (if through employer or other group), agent

☐ Investments
- Stocks: Company, name on certificates, number of shares, certificate numbers, purchase price and date, and location of certificates
- Bonds/notes/bills: Issuer, issued to, face amount, bond number, purchase price and date, maturity date, and location of certificates
- Mutual funds: Company, name on account, number of shares or units, and location of statements and certificates
- Other investments: For each investment, list amount invested, to whom issued, maturity date, issuer, and other applicable data, and location of certificates and other vital papers

☐ Household Contents
- List of contents with name of owners, form of ownership, and location of documents, inventory, and appraisals

☐ Automobiles
- For each car: Year, make, model, color, identification number, title in name(s) of, and location of title and registration

☐ Important Warranties and Receipts
- Location and description

☐ Doctors' Names, Addresses, and Telephone Numbers
- Including dentist, and children's pediatrician and dentist

☐ Checking Accounts
  - Name of bank, name on account, account number, and location of passbook (or receipt) for all accounts

☐ Credit Cards
  - For each card: company (including telephone and address), name on card, number, and location of card

☐ House, Condo, or Co-Op
  - About the home: in whose name, address, legal description, other descriptions needed, lawyer at closing, and locations of statement of closing, policy of title insurance, deed, and land survey
  - About the mortgage: held by, amount of original mortgage, date taken out, amount owed now, method of payment, and location of payment book, if any (or payment statements)
  - About life insurance on mortgage: policy number, location of policy, and annual amount
  - About property taxes: amount and location of receipts
  - About the cost of house: initial buying price, purchase closing fee, other buying costs (real estate agent, legal, taxes), and home improvements
  - About improvements: what each consisted of, cost, date, and location of bills
  - For renters: lease location and expiration date

☐ Funeral Preferences
  - Specify whether *or not* you would like to have any of the following done: Donate organs, autopsy if requested, simple arrangements, embalming, public viewing, least expensive burial or cremation container, or immediate disposition. Remains should be: donated (details of arrangements made), cremated (and the ashes: scat-

tered, buried at), disposed of as follows (details), or buried (at)

- Specify which of the following services should be performed: memorial (after disposition), funeral (before disposition), or graveside to be held at: church, mortuary, or other
- Specify where memorial gifts should be given or whether to omit flowers
- If prearrangements have been made with a mortuary, give details

☐ Signature and date

APPENDIX C

$

Estate Planning Action Plan Worksheet

The following action plan is designed to help you jump-start your estate planning.

ESTATE PLANNING ACTION PLAN

| CURRENT STATUS | | |
NEEDS ACTION	OK OR NOT APPLICABLE	
		1. Decide how you want your estate to be distributed.
		2. Have an attorney prepare a will that is consistent with your personal wishes and circumstances.
		3. Name an appropriate executor.
		4. Establish a durable power of attorney or living trust that protects you in the event of incapacity.
		5. Prepare and keep up-to-date a letter of instructions.
		6. Designate guardians for your children and, if applicable, disabled adults.

CURRENT STATUS

NEEDS ACTION	OK OR NOT APPLICABLE	
		7. Prepare a living will and a health care proxy.
		8. Prepare an estimate of your taxable estate so that you can determine the type of estate planning techniques that will be appropriate.
		9. Make sure sufficient cash will be able to be raised from your estate to meet the needs of your survivors; if not, take appropriate action to increase your estate liquidity.
		10. Make sure that the title in which you hold property (single name, jointly with your spouse, etc.) is appropriate for estate planning purposes.
		11. Any gifts to relatives and/or charitable contributions should take into consideration your financial condition and overall estate planning objectives.
		12. If you own property in more than one state, take appropriate action to minimize eventual probate problems.
		13. Consider the use of revocable and irrevocable trusts as part of your estate planning.
		14. If you own your own business, make provisions for its disposition in the event of your death.
		15. Inform your family and any other beneficiaries of your plans.

Comments:

_____

_____

_____

APPENDIX D

— $ —

Letter of Instructions Worksheet

LETTER OF INSTRUCTIONS

A letter of instructions is an informal document that tells your survivors what to do upon your death. The work sheet that follows will help you figure out what to tell your survivors so that they can make your funeral arrangements and settle your other affairs as you wish. A letter of instructions is not a substitute for a will: you should treat it as a supplement to your will. Unlike your will, a letter of instructions—which is not legally binding—can be easily changed and updated.

EXPECTED DEATH BENEFITS

1. From employer:

   • Person to contact: _____ Telephone: (___) _____

   • Life insurance: $ _____

   • Profit sharing: $ _____

   • Pension plan: $ _____

   • Accident insurance: $ _____

   • Other benefits: _____

EXPECTED DEATH BENEFITS *(continued)*

---

2. From insurance companies—total amount: $

3. From Social Security—lump sum plus monthly benefits: $

4. From the Veterans Administration—amount: $
   (Note: The VA must be informed of the death for benefits to be disbursed.)

5. From other sources:

FIRST THINGS TO DO

---

1. Call:

2. Notify employer. Name and telephone:

3. Make arrangements with the funeral home. (See the "Cemetery and Funeral" section.)

4. Request at least 10 copies of the death certificate. (Usually, the funeral director will get them.)

5. Call lawyer. Name and telephone:

6. Provide the following newspapers with obituary information:

7. Contact the local Social Security office. (See the "Social Security" section.)

8. Retrieve and process insurance policies. (Policy locations are listed in the "Life Insurance" section.)

9. Notify the bank that holds the home mortgage.

10. Notify the following acquaintances and organizations:

CEMETERY AND FUNERAL

Cemetery Plot

1. Location:

2. Date purchased: 19

3. Deed number:

4. Location of deed:

5. Other information (e.g., perpetual care):

FACTS FOR THE FUNERAL DIRECTOR
This list should be brought to the funeral home with the cemetery deed, if possible.

1. Full name:

2. Residence:

3. Marital status: Spouse's name:

4. Date of birth: 19   Birthplace:

5. Father's name and birthplace:

6. Mother's maiden name and birthplace:

7. Length of residence in state: In United States:

8. Military record:

   When:
   (Bring veterans discharge papers, if possible.)

9. Social Security number: Occupation:

FACTS FOR THE FUNERAL DIRECTOR *(continued)*

---

10. Life insurance
    (Bring policy if proceeds will be used for funeral expenses.)

  Insurer   Policy Number

SPECIAL WISHES

1.

2.

3.

PERSONAL EFFECTS

The following personal effects should be given to the named person:

  Item   Person

FUNERAL PREFERENCES

1. Donate these organs:

2. Autopsy if doctor or family requests: ☐ Yes   ☐ No

3. Simple arrangements:
   ☐ No embalming
   ☐ No public viewing
   ☐ The least expensive burial or cremation container
   ☐ Immediate disposition

4. Remains should be:
   ☐ Donated: Arrangements made on _____ , 19 ____ with_____
   ☐ Cremated and the ashes   ☐ Scattered   ☐ Buried at_____
   ☐ Disposed of as follows:_____
   ☐ Buried at_____

5. The following services:
   ☐ Memorial (after disposition)
   ☐ Funeral (before disposition)
   ☐ Graveside
   To be held at: ☐ Church   ☐ Mortuary   ☐ Other:

6. Memorial gift to: Omit flowers: ☐ Yes   ☐ No

7. Prearrangements have been made with the following mortuary:

LOCATION OF PERSONAL PAPERS

1. Last will and testament:

2. Birth and baptismal certificates:

3. Communion, confirmation certificates:

4. School diplomas:

5. Marriage certificate:

LOCATION OF PERSONAL PAPERS *(continued)*

---

6. Military records:

7. Naturalization papers:

8. Other (e.g., adoption, divorce):

SAFE-DEPOSIT BOX
Note: In the event of the death of a safe-deposit box owner, state law may require the bank to seal the deceased's box as soon as notified of the death, even if the box is jointly owned.

---

1. Bank name and address:

2. In whose name: Number:

3. Location of key:

4. List of contents (if extensive, attach separate inventory):

POST OFFICE BOX

---

1. Address:

2. Owners:

3. Box number:

4. Location of key or combination:

INCOME TAX RETURNS

---

1. Location of all previous returns (federal, state, local):

2. Tax preparer's name: Telephone:

3. Location of estimated tax file:
   (Check to see if any estimated quarterly taxes are due.)

DOCTORS' NAMES AND ADDRESSES

1. Doctor's name: Telephone:

   Address:

2. Dentist's name: Telephone:

   Address:

3. Children's pediatrician's name: Telephone:

   Address:

4. Children's dentist's name: Telephone:

   Address:

CHECKING ACCOUNTS
Attach a separate summary if there are multiple accounts.

1. Bank name and address:

2. Name(s) on account:

3. Account number: Type:

4. Location of passbook (or certificate receipt):

5. Special instructions:

CREDIT CARDS
All credit cards in the deceased's name should be cancelled or converted to
the survivor's name. Provide the following information for each card:

1. Company: Telephone:

   Address:

CREDIT CARDS *(continued)*

---

2. Name on card: Number:

3. Location of card:

LOANS OUTSTANDING
Provide the following information for each loan other than mortgages:

---

1. Bank name and address:

2. Name on loan:

3. Account number:

4. Monthly payment:

5. Location of papers and payment book (if any):

6. Collateral (if any):

7. Is there life insurance on the loan?   ☐ Yes   ☐ No

DEBTS OWED TO THE ESTATE

---

1. Debtor:

2. Description:

3. Terms:

4. Balance: $

5. Location of documents:

6. Comments on loan status/discharge:

SOCIAL SECURITY

1. Name: Number:

   Location of Social Security cards:

2. File a claim immediately to avoid possibility of losing any benefit checks. Call local Social Security Administration (SSA) office for appointment and follow SSA's instructions as to what to bring. SSA telephone:

3. Expect a lump sum of about $_____ , plus continuing benefits for children under age 18, or for full-time students until age 22. A spouse may receive benefits until children reach age 18, between ages 50 and 60 if disabled, or if over age 60.

LIFE INSURANCE
To collect benefits, a copy of the death certificate must be sent to each insurance company. Provide the following information for each policy:

1. Policy number: Amount: $

2. Location of policy:

3. Whose life is insured:

4. Insurer's name and address:

5. Kind of policy:

6. Beneficiaries:

7. Issue date: , 19   Maturity date: , 19

8. How paid out:

9. Other options on payout:

10. Other special facts:

LIFE INSURANCE *(continued)*
---

11. For $_____ in veterans insurance, call the local Veterans
Administration office.
Telephone:

OTHER INSURANCE

Accident

1. Insurer's name and address:

2. Policy number:

3. Beneficiary:

4. Coverage:

5. Location of policy:

6. Agent (if any):

HOMEOWNERS/RENTERS AND AUTOMOBILE
Provide the following information for each policy:

1. Coverage:

2. Insurer's name and address:

3. Policy number:

4. Location of policy:

5. Term (when to renew):

6. Agent (if any):

MEDICAL
Provide the following information for each policy:

1. Coverage:

2. Insurer's name and address:

3. Policy number:

4. Location of policy:

5. Through employer or other group:

6. Agent (if any):

HOUSE, CONDO, OR CO-OP
Contact the local tax assessor for documentation needed or for more information.

1. In whose name:

2. Address:

3. Lot: Block: On map called:

4. Other descriptions needed:

5. Lawyer at closing:

   Address:

6. Location of statement of closing, policy of title insurance, deed, land survey, and the like:

7. Mortgage:

   a. Held by:

HOUSE, CONDO, OR CO-OP *(continued)*

---

   b. Amount of original mortgage: $

---

   c. Date taken out: , 19

---

   d. Amount owed now: $

---

   e. Method of payment:

---

   f. Location of payment book, if any (or payment statements):

---

   g. Is there life insurance on mortgage?   ☐ Yes   ☐ No

      • If so, policy number:

      • Location of policy:

      • Annual amount: $

---

8. House taxes

---

   a. Amount: $

---

   b. Location of receipts:

---

9. Cost of house

---

   a. Initial buying price: $

---

   b. Purchase closing fee: $

---

   c. Other costs to buy (e.g., real estate agent, legal, taxes):

---

   d. Improvements: Total: $

---

10. House improvements
    Provide the following information for each improvement:

    a. Improvement:

    b. Cost: $ Date: , 19

    c. Location of bills:

11. If renting, is there a lease: ☐ Yes   ☐ No

    a. Lease location:

    b. Expiration date: , 19

HOUSEHOLD CONTENTS

1. Name of owners:

2. Form of ownership:

3. Location of documents:

4. Location of inventory:

5. Location of appraisals:

AUTOMOBILES
Provide the following information for each car:

1. Year, make, and model:

2. Body type:

3. Cylinders:

4. Color:

AUTOMOBILES *(continued)*

---

5. Identification number:

6. Title in name(s) of:
   Title to automobiles held in the deceased's name must be changed.

7. Location of papers (e.g., title, registration):

IMPORTANT WARRANTIES AND RECEIPTS

Item   Location

INVESTMENTS
Provide the following information (if necessary, attach a separate sheet):

Stocks

1. Company:

2. Name on certificate(s):

3. Number of shares: Certificate number(s):

4. Purchase price and date:

5. Location of certificate(s):

Bonds, Notes, and Bills

1. Issuer:

2. Issued to:

3. Face amount: $ _____   Bond number: _____

4. Purchase price and date: _____

5. Maturity date: _____

6. Location of certificate: _____

Mutual Funds

1. Company: _____

2. Name on account: _____

3. Number of shares or units: _____

4. Location of statements, certificates: _____

Other Investments
For each investment, list the amount invested, to whom it is issued, the issuer, the maturity date, other applicable data, and the location of certificates and other vital papers.

_____

_____

_____

_____

_____

_____

_____

APPENDIX E

$

Estate Planning Questionnaire

The following should make it easier for you to create an effective estate plan. Your goal is to make it as easy as possible for your loved ones to activate your estate plan. To ensure that your plan achieves this goal in fact as well as in spirit, review the following and revise your current plan accordingly.

ESTATE PLANNING

	YES	NO	NA
1. Have you clearly articulated your wishes regarding the ultimate disposition of your estate?			
2. Do you have an up-to-date will that is consistent with your personal wishes and individual circumstances?			
3. Have you named an appropriate executor?			
4. Have you designated an appropriate adult to be responsible for your financial affairs should you become incapacitated?			

	YES	NO	NA
5. Have you prepared a living will and health care proxy?			
6. Has an estimate been made of the size of your taxable estate?			
7. Have you calculated the impact of both federal estate taxes and state death taxes on your estate?			
8. Have provisions been made to provide adequate cash reserves upon your death to provide for your family?			
9. Have you made appropriate provisions in your overall estate planning for property owned in other states?			
10. Are trusts included in your current plan?			
11. Have the effects of current tax regulations on estate planning been evaluated and incorporated into your plan?			
12. Have you informed your family about your funeral plans?			
Comments:			

Will Preparation Checklist

WILL PREPARATION CHECKLIST

THE FOLLOWING ITEMS SHOULD BE INCLUDED IN A WILL:

	Your full name and location of principal residence.
	Statement that the document is a will.
	Date.
	Statement revoking all previous wills.
	Instructions with respect to disposal of your body and funeral arrangements.
	Specific bequests with provisions for the death of the named beneficiaries. Specific bequests are for the transfer of a particular piece of property to a named beneficiary.
	General bequest, which does not specify from which part of the estate the property is to be taken, with provisions for the death of the named beneficiaries.
	Instructions for dividing the residuary, which is the amount of the estate remaining after these specific and general bequests have been made.

Provisions for trusts, including the names of selected trustees and successor trustees.

Statement of who should be presumed to have died first (either husband or wife) should both die in a common accident. This allows both wills to be processed without undue complications or tax effects.

Names of guardians and alternate guardians for minor children, if necessary, or for a handicapped adult, child, or other relative under your care.

Designation of what resources or assets are to be used to pay death taxes.

Names of the executor and substitute executor.

Signature. The will should be signed in the presence of all of the witnesses.

Any major changes in the form of codicils. These, too, must be witnessed and signed, as was the original will.

Comments:

_____

_____

_____

GLOSSARY

adjusted gross income This is your bottom-line income on which your federal income tax is computed. It's computed by subtracting certain expenses and other allowable adjustments (e.g., contributions to IRAs) from your gross income.

alimony Funds paid to an ex-spouse as required by a legally binding separation agreement or divorce decree. Alimony is taxable income to the partner who receives it.

American Depository Receipts (ADRs) Receipts for shares of foreign-based companies traded on U.S. stock exchanges. ADRs, or dollar-dominated securities, are the equivalent of a certain number of company shares.

annuity This is a type of investment in which you or your husband, as policyholders, make payments to an insurance company. The money grows tax-free until you withdraw it at retirement. It earns interest and also pays a death benefit.

asset What you actually own, such as your home, a car, jewelry, and anything else that has monetary value.

asset allocation This is how you apportion your investments in your portfolio. You might own a mix of, say, international mutual funds, large-company stock funds, bonds, and money market funds.

asset management account A type of brokerage or bank account that combines several types of accounts. It might include a brokerage account, a savings account, and a checking account, for example.

balanced mutual funds These are mutual funds invested in a mix of stocks and bonds, usually 60% in stocks and the remainder in bonds.

balance sheet This is a record of your assets, liabilities, and subsequent net worth at a particular time.

beneficiary A person you designate in your will, insurance policy, or retirement plan to receive funds, assets, or proceeds when you die.

blue chip stocks These are shares of well-known companies with solid financial histories and reputations of steady earnings and dividends.

bond rating This is the safety value of a particular bond as assigned by independent agencies, such as Standard & Poor's, that evaluate the possibility of default (that is, whether you will actually get the principal and interest when you are supposed to).

bonds This is the debt of a corporation or the government. A bond buyer provides money to the institution, which in turn pays back the sum with interest at a specified time.

brokerage An intermediary between buyers and sellers of stocks and other securities (e.g., firms like Merrill Lynch). There are three basic levels of brokerages. *Low-commission discount brokers* offer little or no advice, but are an inexpensive way to go. *Full-service brokers* help you make decisions and provide research materials and plenty of hand-holding, but you pay for it. *On-line* brokers are the bargain basement and simply let you execute a trade over your computer without even talking to a person.

capital gain or loss   This is the amount you lose or make from selling one of your assets like your home.

cash-value life insurance   A combination life insurance policy and savings plan. There are several types, including whole life, universal life, and variable life.

certificate of deposit (CD)   This is an insured bank deposit with a guaranteed interest rate that is held for a set time period, usually three months, six months, one year, or five years.

certified financial planner (CFP)   The designation for financial planners who are certified by the CFP Board of Standards in Denver. A CFP must complete a series of courses and continuing education credits on an annual basis.

chartered financial consultant (ChFC)   Designation awarded to qualified financial planners by the American College in Bryn Mawr, Pennsylvania.

chartered life underwriter (CLU)   This is a designation given to qualified life insurance agents by the American College.

child support   Monthly payments, required by state law, that a noncustodial parent must provide to support his or her children. These are not taxable payments.

COBRA   The Consolidated Omnibus Reconciliation Act (COBRA) is a federal law that requires your spouse's company health plan to continue to offer you and any dependents coverage for at least 18 months if you have been divorced or separated or if your spouse has died. You must pay the premiums. You have 60 days to decide to stay on your husband's plan.

common-law property Property divided according to who has title to the asset.

common stock These are equity shares in any publicly traded company.

community property Property and assets accumulated during your marriage are divided equally between the two divorcing parties. Property acquired before the marriage or inherited is excluded. Community-property states are Arizona, California, Idaho, Louisiana, Nevada, New Mexico, Texas, Washington, and Wisconsin.

compounding This is the combination of your principal investment and the subsequent interest it earns that keeps the pot growing month to month and year to year. The more the money compounds, the more interest your investment earns.

credit record This is your permanent record, so to speak, of your financial health as far as lenders are concerned. Every late payment, missed payment, and credit applied for is noted and recorded for at least seven years. A bad credit rating can make it hard for you to get a loan, land a job, or even open a bank account.

cyclical stocks These are shares of companies whose earnings move up and down with the economy, such as carmakers and home builders.

deductible This is the amount you will pay under an insurance plan before the insurer picks up the tab.

defined benefit plan This is a traditional pension plan in which an employer uses a formula based on salary and years of employment with the firm to devise an income to be paid to the employee or beneficiary on a regular basis at retirement.

disability insurance This is insurance coverage that pays benefits if you are unable to work for a period of time due to physical or emotional problems.

diversification   Spreading your investment risk across many different types of investments to mitigate risk.

dividends   Payouts to shareholders by a corporation based on a percentage of its earnings (may be in the form of cash or additional shares).

dollar cost averaging   A method whereby you invest a fixed amount of money at preset intervals, regardless of price per share.

Dow Jones averages   The Dow Industrial, Composite, Transportation, and Utility averages are indicators of how the stock market is faring. The Industrial consists of 30 major stocks such as Disney and IBM. There are 20 stocks in the Transportation average and 15 stocks in the Utility average. The Composite consists of 65 stocks that are a combination of the others.

durable power of attorney   Legal document by which you empower someone to handle your financial affairs if you are incapacitated but still alive.

equitable distribution   This is the basic method of distributing property in 40 states plus the District of Columbia. A court decides how to divide the assets of your marriage based on criteria such as need, earnings potential, and financial contribution to the marriage.

estate plan   This is your blueprint for the orderly disposition of your assets when you die. This should include writing a will, naming a guardian for your children, and designating an executor to handle your affairs. It should also address tax planning to minimize the tax burden levied on your estate.

estate taxes   These are the taxes levied by federal and state governments on a deceased's assets.

executor   This is the individual named in a will to handle the settlement of the estate.

401(k) plan   This is a company's retirement benefit plan that allows employees to make regular, tax-deferred contributions from their salaries each pay period. Companies may match a portion of the employees contributions.

403(b) plan   Similar to a 401(k), these plans are offered to public employees and people who work for nonprofit organizations.

growth mutual funds   Mutual funds that invest in company stocks that are likely to appreciate over time. Capital gains is their objective.

guaranteed investment contracts (GICs)   Investments offered by insurers that guarantee a fixed-income return of around 5%, usually for a period of seven years. These are generally offered as part of 401(k) plans.

guardian   This is the person you select to take care of your children if they are under age 18 when you die.

health care proxy   A legal document in which you designate a person to make medical decisions for you if you are unable to do so. It can be paired with a living will.

income funds   Mutual funds that invest their assets mostly in corporations (such as utilities) that pay dividends.

index funds   Mutual funds that attempt to replicate a certain established stock index like the S & P 500.

individual retirement account (IRA)   A tax-deferred pension plan that allows you to invest up to $2,000 annually, $4,000 if married filing jointly, in an account that is tax-free until you withdraw the money at retirement. There is a penalty for removing the funds before age 59½, and you must start withdrawing the money by age 70½.

international funds   These are mutual funds that invest in stocks of non-U.S. firms. Some invest in only one country or in a specific region.

investment club   A group of people who research stock investments and pool their money together to invest regularly as one entity.

junk bonds   Bonds that are issued by corporations whose financial health is somewhat questionable. There is a clear risk that they may be unable to repay your principal. As a result, the yields they offer are higher than bonds with top ratings.

Keogh plan   This is a type of tax-deferred retirement plan for small-business owners or self-employed people. Up to 25% of income can be put into such a plan.

liability   This is what you owe.

liquidity   This is the measure of how fast you can get your money back from an investment. Treasuries and money markets are considered to be highly liquid. Real estate, on the other hand, is not.

living trust   This is a revocable trust that you establish while you are still living to make sure your assets are managed properly if you are disabled and unable to do so yourself.

living will   A legal document that spells out just how much medical intervention you desire if you have a terminal illness.

load funds   These are mutual funds that levy an up-front sales charge, or commission, when you buy or sell. Most load funds are sold by full-service brokers.

margin accounts   These are brokerage accounts that let you borrow against the value of the securities in your account to make additional investments. You can typically borrow up to 50% of the value of the stocks you own and 90% of the bonds.

maturity   This is the date at which a bond must be paid in full.

mediation A divorce process in which you and your soon-to-be ex hire a professional divorce mediator to work out your agreement. A lawyer will have to finalize the deal.

money market A federally insured bank account that typically pays higher interest than a regular savings account and requires a minimum investment.

money market fund A mutual fund that invests only in short-term securities and is highly liquid.

municipal bonds Bonds issued by a local or state government and sold in denominations of $1,000 and $5,000. The interest from these bonds is free of federal and (usually) local and state taxes.

mutual funds A selection of stocks and bonds, or a mixture of investments, that are pooled together, sold as shares to individual investors, and managed by a professional money manager.

National Association of Securities Dealers (NASD) A membership association of brokerage firms and stock underwriters in the United States. They adhere to ethics guidelines, strict industry procedures, and disciplinary actions for rules violations.

net asset value The market value of a mutual fund share. The value is the total of all the fund's shares minus any liabilities divided by the number of outstanding shares.

net worth Your assets minus your liabilities.

no-load funds Mutual funds that do not charge sales commissions when you buy or sell.

personal financial specialist This is the financial planning designation given to accountants approved by the American Institute of Certified Financial Accountants, which is headquartered in New York.

prenuptial agreement A legally binding agreement signed before marriage that spells out how your assets and your spouse's will be divided in the event of death or divorce.

qualified domestic relations order   This is the state domestic relations court order requiring that an employee's retirement plan must be divided between an employee, a spouse, and any children if there is a divorce.

rate of return   This is how much your invested money is likely to make in a given period of time.

risk   This is a measure of possible loss in value. Generally speaking, the riskier the investment, the higher return it is likely to have.

sector funds   Mutual funds that buy stocks in just one industry, such as autos or biotechnology.

Securities and Exchange Commission (SEC)   The SEC is the federal agency assigned to regulate the securities industry and protect investors from fraudulent activities.

SEP-IRA   A retirement plan for the self-employed, known as the Simplified Employee Pension (or SEP), plan, in which an IRA is opened and up to 13 percent of net earnings can be contributed tax-deferred until retirement.

socially conscious funds   Mutual funds that buy shares only in firms that do not conflict with certain social priorities. For example, they might avoid companies that sell tobacco-related products or choose companies with excellent environmental records.

social security   These are the retirement funds paid by the federal government, provided you have been employed for at least 40 quarters.

stocks   These are shares in a company that are sold to raise capital. There are more than 8,000 publicly traded companies.

term life insurance   This is straight life insurance with no extra cash value. You receive the benefit when your spouse dies.

treasury bill   This is a short-term debt instrument issued by the federal government. The bills mature in periods of three months, six months, or one year. Your minimum purchase is $10,000.

treasury bond   This is a long-term debt instrument, issued by the federal government, that matures in 10 to 30 years. The bonds sell in denominations of $1,000 and pay interest twice a year.

treasury note   This is a medium-term debt instrument, issued by the federal government, that matures in 1 to 10 years. The minimum purchase is $5,000 for under four years; over four years, it's $1,000. Interest is paid twice a year.

universal life insurance   This is a type of insurance in which part of the premium goes toward buying insurance and the remainder is invested.

U.S. savings bonds   Series EE bonds are issued by the federal government. You can purchase them through most banks, credit unions, and S&Ls. All interest is free of state and local taxes.

vesting   When employers offer 401(k) accounts to employees, they typically match a percentage of the employees' contributions. But those employer-provided funds are not awarded to the employee for a set number of years of employment, usually five, which is the vesting period.

will   A legal document stating how you want your assets to be dispersed following your death and naming a guardian for minor children.

wrap account   A plan offered by brokerages and banks that charges investors one annual fee to provide a professional money manager to help manage all your investments.

zero-coupon bond   A bond that sells at a steep discount from its face value and pays no interest until it matures, at which time you can redeem it at the full face value.

INFORMATION RESOURCES

———————— $ ————————

Here's a list of resources for more information that can help you manage your money.

Consumer Watchdogs

Consumer Federation of America: 202-387-6121

Employee Benefit Research Institute: A nonprofit group that offers information on employee benefits: 202-659-0670; 2121 K Street NW, Suite 600, Washington, DC 20037

National Center for Financial Education: http://www.nccfe.org; 619-239-1401

Pension Rights Center: A nonprofit advocacy group that offers information concerning pension problems, divorce, and surviving spouse benefits: 202-296-3776; 918 16th Street NW, Suite 704, Washington, DC 20006-2902

Credit Bureaus

Equifax: 800-685-1111

Experian: 800-682-7654

Trans Union: 800-888-4213

Financial Planners and Advisors

American Institute of Certified Public Accountants:
800-862-4272

Certified Financial Planner Board of Standards:
888-237-6275

Institute of Certified Financial Planners:
800-282-7526

The International Association for Financial Planning:
800-945-4237

National Association of Insurance Commissioners:
816-842-3600

National Association of Personal Financial Advisors:
800-366-2732

National Association of Securities Dealers: 800-289-9999

North American Securities Administrators:
202-737-0900; http://www.nasaa.org

Financial Publications On-Line

Bank Rate Monitor: http://www.brm.com

Barron's: http://www.barrons.com

Bloomberg: http://www.bloomberg.com

Business Week: http://www.businessweek.com

Forbes Magazine: http://www.forbes.com

Fortune Magazine: http://www.pathfinder.com

Investors Business Daily: http://www.ibd.com

Kiplinger's: http://www.kiplinger.com

Money magazine: http://pathfinder.com

Mutual Funds Magazine: http://www.mfmag.com

Smart Money: http://www.smartmoney.com

USA Today: http://www.usatoday.com/money

Worth: http://www.worth.com

Government Sources
The Bureau of Public Debt: 202-874-4000

Internal Revenue Service: http://www.irs.ustreas.gov

Social Security Administration: 800-772-1213;
  http://www.ssa.gov

U.S. Securities and Exchange Commission: 202-942-8088;
  http://www.sec.gov

U.S. Treasury: http://www.ustreas.gov/treasury

Individual Investor Research and Advice
American Association of Individual Investors: 312-280-0170;
  http://www.aaii.com; 625 North Michigan Ave., Suite
  1900, Chicago, IL 60611

American Society of Appraisers: 800-272-8258

Estate Planning Specialists: 800-223-9610

Invest-o-rama: http://www.investorama.com

Morningstar: http://www.morningstar.net

Morningstar Mutual Funds Rating Service: 800-876-5005

Mutual Fund Education Alliance: 816-454-9422; 100
  Northwest Englewood Rd. Suite 130, Kansas City, MO
  64118

Mutual Funds Magazine: http://www.mfmag.com

National Association of Investors Corp: 248-583-6242;
  http://www.better-investing.org; P.O. Box 220, Royal Oak,
  MI 48068-0220

No-Load Stock Insider: 800-233-5922

Value Line: 800-825-8354

Insurance

A.M. Best: 908-439-2200

Ameritas: 800-552-3553

Insurance Information Institute: 800-331-9146

Insurance Quote Services Inc.: 800-972-1104

Moody's Investor's Service: 212-553-0377

Quotesmith: 800-556-9393

SelectQuote: 800-343-1985

Standard & Poor's: 212-208-1527

TermQuote: 800-444-8376

USAA: 800-531-8000

USAA Life: 800-531-8000

Weiss Group: 800-289-9222

Mutual Funds On-Line

Calvert Group: http://www.calvertgroup.com

Charles Schwab: http://www.schwab.com

Fidelity Investments: http://www.fidelity.com

Gabelli Funds: http://www.gabelli.com

T. Rowe Price: http://www.troweprice.com

The Vanguard Group: http://www.vanguard.com

On-Line Banks and Brokers

Accutrade: http://www.accutrade.com

American Express InvestDirect: 800-297-8800;
  http://www.americanexpress.com

Atlanta Internet Bank: http://www.atlantabank.com;
   or 888-256-6932

Discover Brokerage:
   http://www.discoverbrokerage.com

DLJ Direct: http://www.dljdirect.com

e.Schwab: http://www.schwab.com

E*Trade Securities: http://www.etrade.com

1st Source Bank: http://www.1stsource.com

Jack White & Co.: http://www.jackwhiteco.com

MBNA America: 800-577-3556

Quick & Reilly: http://www.quick-reilly.com

Telebank: 800-638-2265

On-Line Financial Sources
Daily Stocks: http://www.dailystocks.com

FinanCenter: http://www.financenter.com

Microsoft Investor: http://www.investor.msn.com

PC Quote: http://www.pcquote.com

Quicken: http://www.quicken.com

StockMaster: http://www.stockmaster.com

Yahoo!Finance: http://www.yahoo.com

Stock Exchanges
American Stock Exchange: 212-306-1000

National Association of Securities Dealers: 800-289-9999;
   http://www.nasdr.com

New York Stock Exchange: 212-656-3000

Other

American Association of Retired Persons: 202-434-2277

National Center for Women and Retirement Research: 800-426-7386

READING RESOURCES

There are hundreds of books dedicated to investing and personal finance topics. Here is a selection that I have found useful and reader-friendly. Happy learning and reading.

American Association of Individual Investors. *The Individual Investors Guide to Computerized Investing*, AAII, 1996. For more information, call 800-428-2244, or write 625 North Michigan Avenue, Department CI, Chicago, Ill. 60611.

American Association of Retired Persons. *The Social Security Book: What Every Woman Absolutely Needs to Know*, 1996. This is a booklet published by AARP. For a copy, write to the organization at 6011 E Street, NW Washington DC 20049.

Armstrong, Alexandra and Mary A. Donahue. *On Your Own: A Widow's Passage to Emotional & Financial Well-Being*, 2nd edition. Dearborn Financial Publishing, 1996.

Berger, Esther, *Money Smart Divorce: What Women Need to Know About Money and Divorce*, Simon & Schuster, 1996.

Bernstein, Peter, ed. *The Ernst and Young Tax Guide*, Wiley, 1998.

Bertrand, Marsha. *A Woman's Guide to Savvy Investing: Everything You Need to Know to Protect Your Future,* AMACOM, 1997.

Brouwer, Kurt, and Stephen Janachowski. *Mutual Fund Mastery: Wealth-Building Secrets from America's Investment Pros,* Times Business, 1997.

Card, Emily, with Christie Watts Kelly, *The Single Parent's Money Guide: A Blueprint for Managing Your Money When You're the Only One Your Family Can Count On.* Macmillan, 1996.

Carlson, Charles. *No-Load Stocks: How to Buy Your First Share & Every Share Directly from the Company—With No Broker's Fee,* McGraw-Hill, 1997.

Carlson, Charles. *60-Second Investor: 201 Tips, Tools, and Tactics for the Time-Strapped Investor,* McGraw-Hill, 1997.

Crane, Peter. *Mutual Fund Investing on the Internet: The Ultimate Guide to Mutual Fund Trading and Information Online,* A Professional, 1997.

Detweiler, Gerri. *The Ultimate Credit Handbook: How to Double Your Credit, Cut Your Debt, and Have a Lifetime of Great Credit,* Plume, 1997.

Eisenberg, Richard, and the editors of *Money* magazine. *The Money Book of Personal Finance,* Warner Books, 1996.

Hannon, Kerry. *10-Minute Guide to Retirement for Women,* Macmillan Spectrum, 1996.

Investment Company Institute. *A Guide to Mutual Funds,* 1997. This is a pamphlet published by the ICI. For a copy, write to ICI at 1401 H Street, NW, Suite 1200, Washington, DC 20005-2148.

Kehrer, Daniel. *Kiplinger's 12 Steps to a Worry-Free Retirement,* Times Books, 1995.

Lynch, Peter, with John Rothschild, *Beating the Street,* Fireside, 1994.

Lynch, Peter, with John Rothschild, *One Up on Wall Street: How to Use What You Already Know to Make Money in the Market* Penguin, 1990.

Mercer, William M. Inc., *Mercer Guide to Social Security and Medicare,* 1997. This guide is published annually by the Social Security Division of William M. Mercer, Inc., the nation's leading employee benefits consulting organization. To request a copy, write to the firm at 1166 Avenue of the Americas, New York, NY 10036-2708.

Miller, Theodore. *Kiplinger's Invest Your Way to Wealth: How to Use Stocks, Bonds, Mutual Funds and Real Estate to Accumulate an Extraordinary Amount of Money,* Time Books, 1995.

Mutual Fund Education Alliance. *Investor's Guide to Low-Cost Mutual Funds,* 1996. To obtain a copy, write to The Mutual Fund Education Alliance, Dept. 0148, P.O. Box 419263, Kansas City, MO 64193-0148.

Patterson, Martha Priddy. *The Working Woman's Guide to Retirement Planning, Saving and Investing Now for a Secure Future,* Prentice-Hall, 1993.

Pond, Jonathan. *The New Century Family Money Book: Your Comprehensive Guide to a Lifetime of Financial Security,* Dell, 1995.

Pond, Jonathan. *4 Easy Steps to Successful Investing,* Avon, 1996.

Quinn, Jane Bryant. *Making the Most of Your Money: A Blueprint for Twenty-First Century Success,* Simon & Schuster, 1997.

Savage, Terry. *New Money Strategies for the '90s: Simple Steps to Creating Wealth and Building Financial Security.* HarperBusiness, 1994.

Securities Industry Association. *Your Guide to Understanding Investing,* Lightbulb Press, 1996. This guide can be obtained by writing the SIA at 1401 Eye Street, Washington, DC 20005 or via its Web site at http://www.sia.com.

Weinstein, Grace. *The Lifetime Book of Money Management,* Gale Research, 1993.

Whitiker, Leslie. *The Beardstown Ladies' Common Sense Investors Guide: How We Beat the Stock Market & How You Can, Too,* Hyperion, 1994.

Wiegold, C. Frederic. *The Wall Street Journal Lifetime Guide to Money: Everything You Need to Know About Managing Your Finances—For Every Stage of Your Life,* 1997.

INDEX